Contents

Preface   vi

Acknowledgements   vii

About the Scottish Consumer Council   viii

Introduction   1

Children's rights   5

Parents' responsibilities and rights   8

A   Admission to school   13

         Advice and assistance   15

         Appeals   20

         Attendance and absence   26

B   Bilingual education (including Gaelic)   29

         Boarding accommodation   32

         Books, equipment and materials   34

         Bullying   36

C   Careers education   41

         Children in care   42

         Children's hearings   45

         Choice of school (including placing requests)   51

         Class size and staffing   55

         Clothing and school uniform   59

         Complaints   63

         Consulting children   68

         Consulting parents   71

         Curriculum (what is taught)   75

D   Denominational schools   79

         Devolved school management   82

         Discipline and punishment   84

E Education authorities   87
      Employment of schoolchildren   90
      Equal opportunities (including sex, race and
      disability discrimination)   92
      Examinations and assessment   101
      Exclusion from school   104

F Fees and charges   111
      Finance and funding of education   113
      Financial assistance (including grants and bursaries) 116
      Flexi-schooling   117

G Guidance   119

H Health   123
      Holidays   126
      Home education   128
      Homework   132
      Human rights   133

I Independent schools   137
      Information for parents   141
      Inspections and inspectors' reports   149

L Leaving age   151
      Legal action   152

M Meals and milk   157
      Medical attention   159
      Migrant and other mobile children   161

P Parent-teacher and parents' associations   163
      Post-16 education and lifelong learning   165
      Pre-school education   167
      Property loss and damage   169

R   Religious education and observance   171

        Residential (former "List D") schools   173

S   Safety and supervision   175

        School boards   179

        School buildings   185

        School closures and changes   189

        School development plans   194

        School records   196

        School rules   202

        School starting age (including deferred entry)   203

        The Scottish Parliament and Scottish Executive   204

        Sex education   206

        Special abilities and aptitudes   208

        Special educational needs   210

        Standards in school education   220

T   Teachers' conditions of service   223

        Transport   226

U   Useful addresses   229

Preface

This A-Z offers an easy to use reference to the law on all aspects of children's education in Scotland. It will arm parents, young people and their advisers with the information they need to get the best out of the education system. It will also help teachers and head teachers become familiar with the legal framework within which they operate.

There has been a considerable expansion in the law to do with education since the 1980s. The Education (Scotland) Act 1981 gave parents new rights to written information about their children's schooling, to ask for a choice of school, to appeal against certain education authority decisions, and to be consulted about school closures and certain other changes. More recently, the Standards in Scotland's Schools etc Act 2000 introduced new rights for parents and for children to be consulted about school education. Each of these areas is covered in detail in this A-Z.

There are, however, many other areas of education law, found mainly in the Education (Scotland) Act 1980 but also hidden away in other statutes, that parents may be less aware of but which may still be important to them. In addition there are a number of "grey areas" of education about which the law has relatively little to say, such as what should be taught at school, but which an A-Z of this kind cannot afford to leave out.

Altogether some 67 different education topics are covered in this A-Z, prepared by Sandra McGuire and Iain Nisbet to whom the SCC is greatly indebted. Although the A-Z should not be regarded as an authoritative statement of the law, which only the courts can rule on, we do believe it will be a valuable source of reference for parents in their dealings with the education system. We also think that the A-Z will be of interest to teachers, education officials, teacher educators and anybody else whose work brings them in touch with parents.

Graeme S Millar

Graeme Millar
Chairman, Scottish Consumer Council, 2001

Acknowledgements

The Scottish Consumer Council is indebted to Sandra McGuire and Iain Nisbet of the Govan Law Centre, who drafted the text for the book. We are also deeply grateful to the many people and organisations who took the time to meet with us to discuss the progress of the book and who commented on the draft text, often at short notice. In particular our thanks go to:

Eilish Garland, Edinburgh Advice and Conciliation Service
Judith Gillespie, Scottish Parent Teacher Council
Ann Hill, Scottish School Board Association
Alastair Macbeth
Maurice Plaskow, UK Education Forum
Alison Preuss, Schoolhouse Home Education Association
Kay Stairs, Glasgow City Council
Kay Tisdall, Children in Scotland
CoSLA
The Scottish Executive

The Housing, Education and Local Government Committee of the Scottish Consumer Council oversaw the production of the book. Its members were:

Ann Clark (committee chair)
Jenny Hamilton
John Hanlon
Alex Wright
Martyn Evans (ex-officio)
Graeme Millar (ex-officio)

The admin support for the production of the book was provided by Kirsty Aird and Joanne Davidson of the Scottish Consumer Council.

About the Scottish Consumer Council

The Scottish Consumer Council (SCC) was set up by government in 1975. Our purpose is to make all consumers matter. We do this by putting forward the consumer interest, particularly that of disadvantaged groups in society, by researching, campaigning and working with those who can make a difference to achieve beneficial change.

While producers of goods and services are usually well-organised and articulate when protecting their own interests, individual consumers very often are not. The people whose interests we represent are consumers of all kinds: they may be patients, tenants, parents, solicitors' clients, public transport users, or simply shoppers in a supermarket.

Consumers benefit from efficient and effective services in the public and private sectors. Service-providers benefit from discriminating consumers. A balanced partnership between the two is essential and the SCC seeks to develop this partnership by:

• carrying out research into consumer issues and concerns;

• informing key policy and decision-makers about consumer concerns and issues;

• influencing key policy and decision-making processes;

• informing and raising awareness among consumers.

Introduction

What is this A-Z for?

This is an A-Z guide for parents to the law in Scotland about children's education. It will help you to understand and deal with the sorts of decisions, difficulties or problems you may be faced with in your child's education. You should find answers in this A-Z to a lot of the questions you are likely to ask about your legal responsibilities and rights in education. Not every single problem or difficulty that may arise can of course be covered, mainly because there are no clear-cut answers to many of the questions parents ask. Certain issues, like the safety and supervision of pupils, have not been clearly resolved in a legal sense, and where this is the case, we say so.

The A-Z attempts to:

tell you about your legal responsibilities and rights over a wide range of matters to do with your child's education. It also says what education authorities and schools must do and what they needn't do in connection with that;

indicate what sorts of services and arrangements you can expect to be provided for your child's education over and above what the law requires. A lot of these services and provisions (such as how children are taught at school) are not laid down by law at all, but result from the policies and practices of education authorities or schools;

point to steps you could take on your own or with others to make sure that your legal responsibilities and rights are properly respected, and what to do if they are not. Bear in mind, though, that a lot of matters to do with your child's education are not legally enforceable. Rather, they will depend on the amount of co-operation or goodwill between education authorities, teachers and parents (such as whether or not a school has a school board or a parent-teachers' association).

What's in this A-Z?

The book begins with an explanation of children's rights, and your basic responsibilities and rights as a parent. It then deals with a whole range of topics, presented in alphabetical order. Questions dealt with include:

• Can you be forced to send your child to school?

• Do you have any choice of school?

• Do you have any educational rights if your child is in care?

• What legal rights do school pupils have?

• Must certain things be taught at school?

• Can your child be made to wear school uniform?

• What punishment can schools give to your child?

• Are schools allowed to charge you for anything?

• Can you insist on homework being given?

• What sort of information about schools are you entitled to?

• How much responsibility do schools have for your child's safety?

• Is there anything education authorities must do before they are allowed to close down a school?

• What can happen if the school rules are disobeyed?

• What is your legal position when teachers go on strike?

And many more! Special sections cover getting advice and help, making a complaint and taking legal action. The role and duties of official bodies like the Scottish Executive and education authorities are also covered. Other sections deal with things like the employment of schoolchildren, school inspections, disability, race and sex discrimination, human rights, and special educational needs. For further information about these and other topics, you are referred to various other publications and useful web sites as well. A good background introduction to the Scottish education system can be found in the Parent Zone web site at: www.ngflscotland.gov.uk/parentzone

How to use this A-Z

Topics are arranged alphabetically. If the section you are looking at does not answer your question fully, you may find it is dealt with under other sections. Check the *"see also"* suggestions at the end of each section for cross-references.

Sometimes it is useful to be able to find the relevant Act of Parliament or the Scottish Parliament. References to these are given at the end of most sections. You should be able to get copies of them through The Stationery Office and in most central reference libraries. A useful web site is www.scotland-legislation.hmso.gov.uk, where you will be able to access all legislation since 1996 about education.

A lot of law is too detailed to put into Acts, and is found in regulations (or "statutory instruments") instead. Again these are referred to at the end of many sections. You should be able to get copies of regulations through The Stationery Office or central reference libraries. Again, www.scotland-legislation. hmso.gov.uk will give you internet access to regulations since 1996.

The government also gives guidance, normally called "circulars", to bodies such as education authorities in carrying out various laws, although they cover a lot of non-legal matters as well. Most do not carry the force of law, advising or recommending what should be done, not what must be done. Some circulars, however, contain statutory guidance which does carry the force of law. Circulars themselves should make clear whether they do or not. Circulars are important in giving you an indication about how the government expects particular laws or policies to be put into practice. Relevant ones are, again, given at the end of sections. You can get copies of circulars from the Scottish Executive.

Sometimes the law can be ambiguous and difficult to interpret. In such cases, it can be useful to see what decisions have been made by the courts (if any). Significant court cases are highlighted throughout the book.

You may wish to find more information about a particular topic, and many sections in this book give you a list of other publications or web sites that can tell you more. Contact details for all of the organisations mentioned in the book are given at the end.

This A–Z should not be regarded as the "last word" in the law – this rests with the courts. You will find a special section about where to go for further advice and help. The Scottish Consumer Council regrets that it cannot itself deal with individual enquiries. Every effort has been made, at the time of going to press, to bring this A–Z up to date with the latest or impending changes in the law, but readers should consult a solicitor or other legal adviser about any further changes in the law since the date of publication.

Children's Rights

The UN Convention on the Rights of the Child

This came into force in 1990 and has been signed by more countries (including the UK) than any other international human rights treaty. The Convention sets out the basic legal rights which should be enjoyed by every child. These include:

- Civil and political rights (such as rights to participation);

- Basic rights to survive and develop (covering health care, education, food and clean water, among others); and

- Protection (such as exploitation of children at work, or discrimination).

By signing the Convention, countries agree to use these basic rights as their minimum standard, and to introduce legislation to remedy gaps in the protection they offer children. Countries have to provide reports on what steps they have taken to comply with the requirements of the Convention. It is not possible however to rely on UN Convention rights in Scottish courts, nor to bring a case against the Scottish or Westminster parliaments for failing to introduce legislation.

The UK has taken steps to comply with the Convention. Probably the most important piece of legislation relating to children since it signed the Convention has been the Children (Scotland) Act 1995. This goes further than any other Act in establishing children as individuals with rights (and responsibilities) of their own, but which reinforces the need for children to have additional protection.

Domestic Law

In many areas of the law (e.g. the law relating to damages and compensation) children have the same rights as adults. So long as they have a sufficient level of understanding, children can consult a solicitor and (if necessary) raise a court action in their own name. Some laws give rights only to a specific group of people, such as parents.

Increasingly, our domestic legislation is giving rights to children, which were previously only enjoyed by adults. An example of this in education is the child's right to appeal against an exclusion from school.

Many of your rights as a parent are only exercisable to promote your child's wellbeing. It would be possible to challenge the actions of a parent in certain circumstances if they had exercised their rights in a way which was not conducive to the welfare of their child, or which was contrary to the specific wishes of their child. A good example of this would be the recent introduction of the right of every child of school age to be provided with school education from the education authority. Although this has not been tested in the courts, this would seem to overrule the parent's right to choose how their child is educated. It could be possible, for example, for a child to go to court to be allowed to attend a local authority school rather than a private one chosen by their parent.

Where to find out more

"UN Convention on the Rights of the Child: a guide for young people" by The Scottish Office (available from the Scottish Executive).

"The UN Convention and Children's Rights in the UK" by Peter Newell (1991). Available from the National Children's Bureau.

"Children (Scotland) Act 1995 Information Pack" by Children in Scotland.

"The Children (Scotland) Act 1995 – Developing Policy and Law for Scotland's Children" by E Kay M Tisdall (1997). Available from The Stationery Office.

"A Children's Rights Commissioner – Research Note" by the Scottish Parliament (August 2000).

Legal references used in this section

Section 1 of the **Standards in Scotland's Schools etc (Scotland) Act 2000**

Parents' Responsibilities and Rights

> "It shall be the duty of the parent of every child of school age to provide efficient education for him suitable to his age ability and aptitude either by causing him to attend a public school regularly or by other means."
>
> "In the exercise and performance of their powers and duties under this Act, the Scottish Ministers and education authorities shall have regard to the general principle that, so far as is compatible with the provision of suitable instruction and training and the avoidance of unreasonable public expenditure, pupils are to be educated in accordance with the wishes of their parents."

Sections 30 and 28 of the Education (Scotland) Act 1980

What are your basic responsibilities?

Parents are legally responsible for making sure that their children are properly educated once they reach school age (approx. 5–16). You normally do this by seeing that your child regularly attends a school run by the education authority. It is possible for your child to be educated at home, at an independent school, or somewhere else instead. The law does not say exactly what sort of education should be provided. It uses the words "efficient education" without saying what this means, except that it should be suitable to your child's age, ability and aptitude.

Your legal responsibilities as a parent continue until your child reaches school leaving age (approx. 16). If your child has special educational needs, some of your legal responsibilities may extend beyond that age.

On reaching school leaving age young people normally become responsible for their own education – unless a learning disability means they are unable to do so. Parents may be expected to contribute towards their maintenance if they decide to carry on at school or college after 16, but grants or bursaries may be available (see **Fees and charges** and **Financial assistance (including grants and bursaries)**).

"Parent" for the purposes of education law includes guardian and anyone who has parental responsibilities for, or has the care of, a child or young person.

What else do parents have to do?

As a parent, you have a number of special legal duties in connection with your child's education. These duties include:

Making sure your child is properly educated, either through regular attendance at school or "by other means", for example by arranging for your child to be educated at home (see **Home education**, **Flexi-schooling**, **Attendance and absence** and **Independent schools**).

Seeing that your child obeys the school rules (see **School rules**).

Making sure that your child attends school adequately and suitably dressed, so they can take advantage of the schooling offered (see **Clothing and school uniform**).

Arranging for your child to be medically, dentally or psychologically examined if asked to do so (see **Medical attention** and **Special educational needs**).

Making proper arrangements for your child's safety and supervision outside school hours.

The basic rights of parents

Parents have the right to choose the kind of education they want for their children, within limits. The education authority only has to "have regard" to your wishes, and does not have to go along with them if it thinks that the instruction you want is unsuitable for your child or that unreasonable expenditure might be needed for extra staff or accommodation. It may also take other things into account.

You also have the right to ask for a choice of school (see **Choice of school**), although your child may have to attend another school under certain circumstances.

Do parents have other rights?

You also have a number of specific rights. If education authorities, and in some cases school staff, fail or refuse to observe them, they risk being taken to court. You have a right to:

Receive certain written information about schools (see **Information for parents**).

Be consulted about school closures and other changes (see **Consulting parents**).

Have your child educated without having to pay fees, although charges may be payable for certain items and some education after school leaving age (see **Fees and charges**).

Be consulted about or appeal against decisions made about your child's special educational needs (see **Special educational needs**).

Appeal if your child faces exclusion from school (see **Exclusion from school**).

Withdraw your child from religious education and observance and from sex education classes (see **Religious education and observance** and **Sex education**).

Have your child taught in Gaelic if you live in a Gaelic speaking area (see **Bilingual education**).

Freedom of your child from race, disability (from September 2002) or sex discrimination (see **Equal opportunities**).

In certain circumstances, receive assistance with clothing, boarding accommodation, meals and milk, transport, grants and other financial assistance (see **Financial assistance (including grants and bursaries)**, **Clothing and school uniform**, and **Meals and milk**).

If you have any problems about services which must be provided by law, it is advisable to discuss them with the school staff first. If this is not satisfactory, you could complain to the school or education authority, or even to the Scottish Ministers (see **Complaints**).

The rest of this book provides detailed information on all of the above-mentioned responsibilities and rights of parents.

Where to find out more

"The Parents' Charter in Scotland" by The Scottish Office (1995). Available from the Scottish Executive.

"Your Children Matter – know your responsibilities and rights" by The Scottish Office (1998). Available from the Scottish Executive.

Legal references used in this section

Sections 5 and 6 of the **Standards in Scotland's Schools etc. (Scotland) Act 2000**

Section 1(3) of the **Children (Scotland) Act 1995**

Sections 1(5); 3; 9; 22; 22A; 22D; 28A; 28I; 28J; 28K; 28H; 30; 31; 32(3); 33(2) & (4); 54; 57(2); and 61(1) of the **Education (Scotland) Act 1980**

Circular no. 2/2001 "Standards in Scotland's Schools etc. Act 2000: Conduct of Sex Education in Scottish Schools."

Reg 4A of the **Schools General (Scotland) Regulations 1975**

ADMISSION TO SCHOOL

Primary school

Most children are admitted to primary school aged either 4 or 5 and transfer to secondary after primary 7. The education authority must tell all parents whose children are due to start primary school the following session about the local school. It must also tell you about your right to choose a different school.

If you have good reason why you would like your child to start school earlier than usual, you can approach the education authority to have your child admitted early to primary school.

Special educational needs

If your child has special educational needs which have been identified at the pre-school stage, you should have been involved in discussions about whether your child's needs would be best met at your local primary, or whether special educational provision is required for your child.

Going from primary to secondary

If your child is due to transfer from primary to secondary at the start of the following session, you will also be told about the local school, and of your right to request a different school.

What if my child is not ready for secondary school?

In some circumstances, you may defer your child's entry to secondary school for a year to allow them to repeat a primary year, if you feel that they would be unable to benefit from secondary education. The education authority may suggest this to you, or you can ask the education authority to consider it. If you think this may be appropriate for your child you should discuss your child's progress with his/her head teacher in the first instance.

Changing school

If you are moving area, your child may need to change school. You should contact the education authority to find out about the local school there. It will also tell you how to go about enrolling your child in the school. Again, if you would prefer your child to attend a different school, you are entitled to make a placing request.

See also

Choice of school
School starting age
Special educational needs

ADVICE AND ASSISTANCE

Where to get advice and assistance

School staff. Your child's class, guidance or head teacher will usually be willing to discuss any concerns you have about your child's schooling. You should always try to discuss concerns about how your child is getting on at school (e.g. their educational progress, or bullying) with school staff before taking the matter any further.

Other parents. Sometimes you can get the information you need just by speaking informally to other parents whose children attend the school. This can be particularly helpful if you are considering what school to send your child to.

Parents' associations or school boards. If there is a PTA/PA or school board at your child's school, they may be able to offer advice on how to deal with a specific query, or may be able to take up a general issue with the school on your behalf.

Education authority officials. If you need information about the education authority's policies or procedures, you can get this by contacting the relevant section of your education department. Many functions such as special educational needs provision, grants, bursaries etc. will be dealt with at this level.

Careers Office. Your local careers office will be able to provide your child with information about employment and further and higher education.

Local Advice Centres. Citizen's Advice Bureaux are staffed by volunteers and paid workers and have access to a range of information materials. They provide a free basic advice service on a whole host of different subjects. They will be able to provide general advice on educational matters. They may be able to write letters on your behalf and some may offer a representation service at appeal committee hearings. Some areas have other advice services. If you have a local community council, they will be able to tell you what advice services are available in your area, or you could check the Yellow Pages. There may be a youth information service in your area, which is likely to have information on schools and education.

Solicitors. Solicitors will be able to provide more detailed and expert legal advice and representation if necessary. Not all solicitors will deal with education matters, so you should ask before making an appointment whether they deal with education law. The Law Society of Scotland has a list of solicitors who have specialist accreditation in child law. They may be most likely to take your case on. Legal advice is available free of charge, or subject to a small contribution to those on low incomes, under the Advice and Assistance scheme. Many solicitors offer a free first interview, where they will establish whether you would be eligible for advice and assistance. Representation at appeal committee hearings is not covered by the Advice and Assistance scheme, and you may be charged a fee for representation there. Law Centres exist to provide free legal advice and representation in areas of unmet legal need, to people living in their areas. If there is a Law Centre in your area, they may be willing to take on an education case. You should contact the Scottish Association of Law Centres to find out if there is a Law Centre in your area.

Other specialist organisations can provide advice in relation to specific areas. For example:

Children in Care	Your child's social worker will be able to give you advice or refer you to someone within the social work department who can deal with a specific enquiry.
Independent Schools	Independent Schools Information Service

	Scottish Council of Independent Schools
Special Educational Needs	Enquire Independent Special Education Advice (ISEA)
Children affected by disability	Enable
Students affected by disability	SKILL: National Bureau for Students with Disability
Home Education	Schoolhouse
Higher Education	Universities and Colleges Admission Service (UCAS)
Financial support for students	Student Awards Agency for Scotland Student Loans Company
Racial Discrimination	Commission for Racial Equality
Sex Discrimination	Equal Opportunities Commission
Disability Discrimination	Disability Rights Commission

Publications and internet materials

There are a wide range of books, periodicals and leaflets on education-related topics. Increasingly, materials are available free of charge on the internet. This is probably the quickest and cheapest way to get up to date information. Most of the organisations above produce leaflets for parents and children. There is also a list of useful addresses and web sites at the end of this book. You can find out what leaflets are available by contacting an organisation directly or by checking their web site if they have one.

You can get copies of the Scottish Executive circulars by contacting the Scottish Executive Education Department. Copies of Inspectors' reports are available from HM Inspectorate of Education. Copies of statutes and regulations are available from HMSO. Details of how to contact these organisations are at the end of the book.

Newspapers such as The Scotsman, The Herald and The Guardian have weekly education pages where current education issues are discussed. These papers will also report on any important developments. You may also find the Times Educational Supplement useful.

Your local library or bookshop will also have a section on education which may have books of interest.

Points to remember

Always try to achieve an amicable solution to any problems. It will usually be in your child's best interests if you, the school and the education department can work together. If there are points of contention, try to keep calm and listen carefully to what is being said. This will help you get a clear idea of the reasoning behind a decision you disagree with.

It is helpful to keep copies of everything you submit in writing, such as application forms and letters. If at a future date you need to seek advice or take action, it is important that you have an accurate record of what you have submitted. You should also keep a note of the names of anyone you speak to on the telephone for ease of reference.

If you are seeking advice, make sure the person you are speaking to has all the facts. Give them all the information you have, even if you don't feel it's particularly relevant.

Finally, try to be patient; it may take some time for your problem to be solved. In many cases, there is no legal remedy available…a change in the law or established procedures may be required.

See also

Complaints
Guidance
Information for parents
Legal action
Parent-teacher and parents' associations
School boards

Where to find out more

See the Parent Zone web site (address at the end of the book).
Scottish Child Law Centre

APPEALS

You can make an appeal about these four main areas of the law:

• Special Educational Needs;

• Placing Requests;

• Exclusions; and

• Attendance Orders.

Who has the right to make an appeal?

You, as the parent, have the right of appeal in all cases where your child is still under school leaving age. You may also have the right of appeal in special educational needs cases where your child is over that age, but doesn't have the necessary understanding to appeal on his/her own.

Where *your child* is over school leaving age, he/she has the right of appeal, and you do not.

In exclusion cases, if your child is twelve or over (or is of sufficient maturity and understanding) but under school leaving age, *you both* have the right to appeal.

What can I appeal about?

There are only certain decisions which can be appealed:

• Exclusion from school;

• The making or amendment of an Attendance Order;

• Refusal of a placing request (but not placing requests for nursery school);

- Recording a pupil or continuing the Record of Needs;

- Refusing to record a pupil or discontinuing the Record of Needs;

- The summary of a pupil's needs in the Record of Needs;

- The statement of the pupil's special educational needs in the Record of Needs; and

- The nominated school in the Record of Needs (but only where you also made a placing request to a different school).

Who do I make the appeal to?

For certain issues, you need to write to your education authority and ask to make an appeal to the Scottish Ministers. For other issues, your appeal will be heard by an education appeal committee organised by your education authority. And in some other instances, you will make your appeal to the sheriff court.

Appeals to the Scottish Ministers

Appeals about the Record of Needs (except for choice of school) are heard by the Scottish Ministers. First of all, you need to write to the education appeal committee (see below) to ask for the appeal. You need to do this within 28 days of the decision you disagree with. The Ministers appoint an advisor to speak to you (and your child) about your appeal and to investigate. The advisor will write a report about your appeal and will send this, together with your views and the education authority's views, to the Scottish Ministers to make a decision. You cannot make a further appeal, although you may be able to take legal action.

The education appeal committee

Appeals about placing requests, nominated schools and exclusions are heard by an education appeal committee, set up by the education authority. Education appeal committees are not education authority committees. They are meant to be independent bodies which are supervised by the Scottish Committee of the Council on Tribunals. They are also subject to investigation by the Commissioner for Local Administration in Scotland (known as the Local Government Ombudsman).

An appeal committee can have three, five or seven members. These will be councillors from the local authority, parents, and others with an interest in education. The councillors must not outnumber the parent members by more than one. The chair must be one of the parent members. None of the members should be involved in the school your child goes to, or has applied to go to.

The appeal committee must tell you when the date for the hearing will be, within fourteen days of receiving your appeal, and must give you at least 14 days warning. The hearing must usually be within 28 days of their receiving your appeal.

You (if you are making the appeal) or your child (if he/she is) have the following rights at an appeal:

• The right to appear and be represented;

• The right to be accompanied by up to three people (including your representative, if any); and

• The right to submit a written case, as well as, or instead of, speaking on your own behalf.

The appeal hearing will almost always go in this order:

• The education authority will present its arguments;

• You can question any of its witnesses;

• You will present your arguments;

• You and/or your witnesses can be questioned;

• The education authority will sum up; and finally

• You have a chance to sum up your case.

The appeal committee must take into account all relevant matters in making its decision. These should include those set out in their Code of Practice.

The appeal committee must give its decision to you in writing within fourteen days, together with the reasons for the decision. It is not enough just to repeat the legal grounds. You should be able to understand why a decision was taken. You must be told about your right of further appeal.

If no reasons are given, you have a right to ask for a statement of reasons for the decision, if you ask at the time the decision is given to you or before. The reasons given for the decision become part of the decision itself. This is important, as it may help you to bring a legal challenge against the decision, either by appeal or by judicial review. "Adequate" reasons must be given, and a failure to provide adequate reasons can be excellent grounds for appeal.

A recent official report about education appeal committees raised serious concerns about inadequate and inconsistent training for chairs, members and clerks of committees (including on human rights); the tendency to uphold the education authority's decision (especially in exclusion cases); and the quality of the decision-making itself.

The education authority has no right of further appeal from the education appeal committee.

"Deemed Decisions"

If an appeal committee has not heard your appeal within one month (for exclusions) or two months (for placing requests); or fails to give you a written decision within fourteen days of the hearing, then it is *deemed* or assumed by law to have decided automatically the case against you. You can then make an appeal to the sheriff court.

Appeals to the sheriff court

For any appeal heard by the appeal committee, you can make a further appeal to the sheriff court. The appeal must be made within 28 days (or later if there is a good reason) by way of "summary application". An appeal against an Attendance Order goes straight to the sheriff court. The law does not say exactly when an appeal should be granted. For placing requests, the appeal is a complete rehearing of the case. For other cases, the court will probably decide whether the education authority can be shown to have used its discretion improperly in some way.

An appeal to the sheriff court, while kept as informal as possible, is a complex legal procedure, and you should seek legal advice and/or representation, from a solicitor familiar with education law. You or your child may be entitled to Legal Aid.

Human Rights

The education appeal committee, the Scottish Ministers and the sheriff court are all covered by the Human Rights Act. This means that, wherever possible, they must interpret the law so that it doesn't breach your (or your child's) human rights. They must also take into account the decisions of the European Court or Commission of Human Rights. For example, the Court has decided that it is a breach of the European Convention on Human Rights to exclude a child from school for the parent's refusal to comply with school rules, if that refusal is due to religious or philosophical convictions. An education appeal committee must take that decision (and others) into consideration if dealing with a similar case. Failure to do so may be an unlawful act, and would be good grounds for appeal.

See also

Attendance and absence
Choice of school
Complaints
Exclusion from school
Human Rights
Legal action
Scottish Executive and the Scottish Parliament
Special Educational Needs

Where to find out more

"Code of Practice for Constitution and Procedures of Education Appeal Committees in Scotland" by CoSLA (Jan 1988).

Scottish Committee of the Council on Tribunals *Annual Report.* The 1999/00 one includes a special report on education appeal committees.

Legal references used in this section

Section 41 of the **Standards in Scotland's Schools etc. (Scotland) Act 2000**

Section 1; 3; 6 of the **Human Rights Act 1998**

Section 10(1); 10(6); 4(3), Schedule 1, Part II, para 50(b) of the **Tribunals and Inquiries Act 1992**

Section 28D(1); 28E(3); 28H(3); Schedule A1 of the **Education (Scotland) Act 1980**

Section 23(2)(f) of the **Local Government (Scotland) Act 1975**

Reg 7(1); 8(1)(a); 8(2); 11(2) of the **Education (Appeal Committee Procedures) (Scotland) Regulations 1982**

Reg 5(1) of the **Education (Placing in Schools) (Scotland) Regulations 1982**

See Kelly v. Dumfries and Galloway Regional Council 1994 GWD 12-763

Campbell and Cosans v. United Kingdom (1982) 4 EHRR 293

ATTENDANCE AND ABSENCE

Attendance at school

There is no *duty* on children to attend school or on their parents to send them to school. What the law requires is that you provide your school-aged child with efficient education suitable to his/her age, ability and aptitude, either by sending him/her to a local authority school, or by some other means. "Some other means" includes educating the child at home or sending him/her to an independent school.

Parents have a legal obligation to seek their child's views when making important decisions such as choosing a particular type of education.

Once your child is registered and attends a local authority school, you must ensure that he/she attends regularly. If you wish to withdraw your child from the school, then you must ask for the education authority's consent. The education authority will make some enquiry into your proposal for education by "some other means", and must not unreasonably withhold its consent to your child being withdrawn from school.

Exemptions from school attendance

In exceptional circumstances, the parents of children over 14 may ask the education authority to exempt their child from attending school for the rest of that school session, in order for the child to help out at home. This would only be granted if the child's home circumstances meant that it would cause "exceptional hardship" if the child had to attend school. If the exemption is granted because of the illness or infirmity of a member of the child's family, then as far as practicable and without undue delay, the education authority must make special arrangements for the child to receive education out of school.

Absence from school

Once your child is registered at and attends a local authority school, they must attend regularly, unless there is a *reasonable excuse* for absence. You have a reasonable excuse if:

- Your child cannot attend school or receive education because of illness (the education authority may arrange for your child to be medically examined in this situation, and you could be prosecuted if you do not allow the examination to take place);

- Your child lives beyond the statutory walking distance from school; or

- There are other circumstances which would count as a reasonable excuse. This depends very much on the facts and circumstances of the individual case, but it would only be in exceptional cases that it could be used.

If one of these applies to your child, you should notify the education authority as soon as possible, and it should make arrangements for your child to receive education outwith school, without undue delay.

Absence without reasonable excuse

If the education authority suspects that you have failed to make sure your child attends school regularly, without reasonable excuse, it can call you to a meeting to discuss the reasons for your child's non-attendance. (This is usually called the attendance council). The attendance council can postpone making a decision for up to 6 weeks, and has the power to:

- prosecute you; and/or

- refer your child to the Reporter to the Children's Panel; and/or

- make an "attendance order" requiring your child to attend the local school.

If you do not agree with the attendance order, you can appeal against it to the Sheriff Court within 14 days of the date the order was served. If you want to appeal against an attendance order, you should seek legal advice. You may be eligible for Legal Aid.

See also

Appeals
Children's hearings
Health
Home education
Independent schools
Transport

Where to find out more

"Attending School: how much does it matter?" Spotlights no. 58 by the Scottish Council for Research in Education.(1996).

Legal references used in this section

Section 14 (as amended); 30 of the **Education (Scotland) Act 1980**.

BILINGUAL EDUCATION (including Gaelic)

Gaelic

Education authorities must provide Gaelic teaching at schools in Gaelic-speaking areas. This (i.e. teaching any subject in the Gaelic language) is mostly provided in schools in the Western Isles, Skye & Lochalsh, and certain parts of the Highlands; but there are now about 60 primary schools offering Gaelic-medium education across Scotland. The Scottish Executive, through Storlann, the National Gaelic Resource Centre, is developing improved teaching materials and steps are being taken to increase the supply of Gaelic-medium teachers.

The education authority must give you written information (in both Gaelic and English, where appropriate) about schools in its area which have Gaelic teaching.

The education authority's annual statement of education improvement objectives must include details of how or in what circumstances it will provide Gaelic-medium education. Where Gaelic-medium education is provided, the education authority must include details of how it will try to develop this.

Other Languages

Your child has no general right to be taught in the language of your choice (or even his/her first language). The European Court of Human Rights decided that the state can insist on teaching being provided in the majority language for the area. Your right to have your child educated in accordance with your own religious or philosophical convictions does not apply to linguistic preference.

Where other languages are widely used in the education authority's area, it must provide its information for parents in those languages if necessary.

The children of "migrant" workers from EU countries have limited rights to some teaching in the host country in their native language. The host country must take appropriate measures to promote, alongside the regular curriculum, the teaching of the mother tongue and culture of the country of origin for these children.

Official guidance recommends that all pupils should have opportunities to reflect upon their own use of language and to develop "a conviction of the worth of their own accents and dialects". It also recommends that teachers should foster "respect for and interest in each pupil's mother tongue and its literature, whether English, Scots, Gaelic, Urdu, Punjabi, Cantonese or any other".

Children with special educational needs or other circumstances which mean they are considered in law to be a "child in need" have additional rights. Services provided by the local authority (including education) must have "due regard" to your child's linguistic background, as far as is practicable. However, your child will not have special educational needs just because of linguistic difference.

See also

Standards in school education

Where to find out more

5-14 National guidelines on the curriculum for schools, available from Learning and Teaching Scotland.

Legal references used in this section

Section 5(2)(c) of the **Standards in Scotland's Schools etc. (Scotland) Act 2000**

Sections 22, 23 and 93 of the **Children (Scotland) Act 1995**

Section 1(5) of the **Education (Scotland) Act 1980**

Reg 13(3); Sched I, Part III (n) of the **Education (School and Placing Information) (Scotland) Regulations 1982**

Article 3 of **Council Directive 77/486/EEC** of 25 July 1977 on the education of the children of migrant workers

Belgian Linguistic Case (no. 2) (1979–80) 1 EHRR 252

BOARDING ACCOMMODATION

When will the education authority provide boarding accommodation?

The education authority must provide boarding accommodation if:

The nearest suitable school is too far for your child to travel to on a daily basis;

Your home is very remote; or

There are other exceptional circumstances which mean your child would be unable to receive the full benefit of school education unless boarding accommodation was provided (for example if your work forces you to be away from home a lot and there is no-one else to look after your child).

If your child attends a particular school as a result of a placing request, then while the education authority *may* provide boarding accommodation, it is not under any obligation to do so.

What type of accommodation can be provided?

Accommodation can be provided in a boarding school, hostel, children's home or other institution, or with a family or individual. If the accommodation is with a family or individual, you have the right to request they are of a particular religious denomination, and the education authority must give effect to your request, as far as reasonably practicable.

When the education authority is making arrangements for your child to receive boarding accommodation, it must consult you.

There is also an obligation on you to take account of your child's views on the matter.

While your child is being accommodated under these provisions, the education authority has a duty to safeguard and promote their welfare, and has the right to carry out inspections to ensure that your child's welfare is adequately safeguarded and promoted.

Do I have to pay?

If the accommodation is provided for the purpose of school education, the education authority cannot charge you for the cost of the board and lodging. It must also provide travel or reimburse the cost of your child's travelling to and from the accommodation.

Religious observance

If you wish your child to be permitted to attend religious worship or receive religious instruction outwith school hours, the education authority must make arrangements for this, provided it incurs no additional expenditure as a result.

See also

Choice of school
Religious education and observance
Special educational needs

Legal references used in this section

Section 50; 52 of the **Education (Scotland) Act 1980**

(B)

BOOKS, EQUIPMENT AND MATERIALS

School Books

Pupils in local authority schools must be provided, free of charge, with any books, writing materials, stationery, mathematical instruments, practice material and other articles, which are necessary for the course of study being followed.

Schools are allocated a budget for materials and have a certain amount of discretion in what is provided, within education authority guidelines. Schools sometimes fundraise or ask for donations to cover the costs of books and other materials, but it is unlawful to require payment from you or your child for essential articles.

Damage to books, equipment and materials

Necessary articles provided by the school free of charge will remain the property of the education authority and may have to remain within the school buildings. If your child is permitted to take school books home, then he/she is responsible for taking care of them and may have to pay if they get damaged.

The education authority can also provide books, printed works and audio-visual media for school pupils. This may be through a central library service or through the public libraries.

Independent schools

If your child goes to an independent or fee-paying school, you will have to pay for the books and materials, either as part of the fees or separately, unless your child's fees are met by the education authority.

See also

Property loss and damage

Legal references used in this section

Section 11(1); 12 of the **Education (Scotland) Act 1980**

BULLYING

Bullying happens in every school. Around 50% of pupils will be victims of bullying at some stage in their schooling. Children can be seriously affected by bullying. It can lead to anxiety, distress, illness, absenteeism and arrested educational development. Bullying has many guises, but verbal and psychological bullying can be every bit as damaging as cuts and bruises.

What is the school's responsibility?

The education authority must provide an "adequate and efficient" education for children in its area. Where education is provided by the authority, it has a duty to make sure that the education is "directed to the development of the personality, talents and mental and physical abilities" of your child to his/her fullest potential.

It has been well established and is now accepted that bullying can have a substantial adverse effect on children's educational development and attainment. If your child is suffering academically as a result of bullying, then your education authority must act in order to fulfil the above duties. The most effective way of doing this would often be to try and resolve the bullying problem, although other measures and support may also be needed. In serious cases, your child may develop recordable special educational needs as a result of bullying.

The education authority must take reasonable care for the safety of pupils under its charge.

What about independent schools?

All schools have to take reasonable care for the safety and health of children in their charge and to exercise care and forethought, and not to subject them to unavoidable risk of harm.

Independent schools are not, however, bound by the same duties as local authorities (as detailed above). You will be in a contractual relationship with the school. There is unlikely to be an express condition that the school will protect your child from bullying. However there may be a term, implied by law, that the school will take reasonable steps to ensure a safe environment in which to learn. That may be especially so where the school has adopted a written anti-bullying strategy, as is recommended by the Scottish Council of Independent Schools. A failure to follow that strategy might amount to a significant breach of contract.

What does the school have to do?

Schools must comply with normal practice for dealing with bullying. There are official guidelines which indicate what this normal practice is (or should be).

The Scottish Executive Education Department (SEED) has provided all Scottish schools with two anti-bullying packs. Many local authorities have also produced their own materials and/or employed key staff to assist schools with the bullying problem.

The SEED anti-bullying packs are now the principal guides for schools in this field. Both strongly recommend that each school has an individual, specific anti-bullying policy. This recommendation is endorsed by the Scottish Executive. HM Inspectorate of Education also now expects schools to have such a policy statement.

It is suggested that the single most effective thing that a school can do to tackle bullying is the adoption of an anti-bullying policy. The policy should outline how the issue will be raised within the school's curriculum, and how incidents will be dealt with after they happen. To be effective, it must involve pupils, parents, teachers and other staff.

Bullying of all kinds should be opposed. There should be a clear message (both in the words of the policy and in its implementation) that bullying is wrong, and will not be tolerated. In many of the most effective examples, punishment is rejected as ineffective or inappropriate. Children who bully others may need as much help as their victims. Schools are increasingly adopting no-blame and peer-support strategies for resolving problems. The aim is to reduce the level of bullying and improve the learning environment.

In this context, failure to follow the guidelines on anti-bullying policies, or failure to follow a policy which has been drawn up may amount to a breach of a duty owed by the school to your child.

Can I keep my child off school?

In some circumstances, your natural obligation to protect your child can override your legal obligation to keep sending him/her to school. However, this does not apply if the school has not been told of the bullying, and has therefore had no opportunity to address the problem.

In both the most recent cases involving bullying in schools, it has been stressed that co-operation with the school by both child and parent(s) is essential. In particular, the courts have taken the view that the child must tell the school about the bullying, and continue to tell until the bullying stops. This is often extremely difficult for the child to do. However, if you or your child do not tell, then the school or education authority will often have no legal duties to stop the bullying.

Should I involve the police?

In June 1997, Sheriff Cameron sentenced two girl pupils of the Nicolson Institute School in Stornoway, Lewis to three months' youth detention for assault on a fellow pupil. Their victim had earlier committed suicide as a result of the assault and other bullying.

Bullying can involve things such as assault, harassment, intimidation, extortion and theft. These are offences, at any age (over 8). All such incidences should be reported to the police. In some areas (such as Lothian & Borders and Grampian), schools and the police are now working together to combat and prevent bullying. If the school has not reported the matter, then you should. If your child has been injured, he/she should be taken to see a medical practitioner so that the injuries can be recorded. If there are witnesses to the incident, the police should be asked to note their statements. As with all bullying, the school should also have kept an independent record of the incident.

Legal Action

Where the school or education authority has breached its duties to your child (as explained above) it would then be legally responsible for any reasonably foreseeable consequences. This means that you (or your child) could take legal action for compensation for injuries (including psychological, emotional or financial injury) sustained as a result of the breach.

You should seek legal advice as soon as possible. You or your child may be entitled to Legal Aid.

See also

Attendance and absence
Independent schools
Legal action
Safety and supervision
Special educational needs

Where to find out more

"*Bullying and the law*" by Iain Nisbet (1998). Available from the Drumchapel Law & Money Advice Centre (check the Scottish Association of Law Centres for the address).

"*Guidelines on Child Protection*" by Kathleen Marshall; 2nd Edition (1997). Available from the Scottish Council of Independent Schools.

"*Bullying at School: Advice for Families*" by the Scottish Council for Research in Education (1997).

"*Let's Stop Bullying: advice for young people*" by the Scottish Executive (1999).

"Let's Stop Bullying: advice for parents and families" by the Scottish Executive (1999).

"Talk About Bullying" by the Scottish Parent Teacher Council.

Childline: Freephone 0800 44 11 11 / 0800 11 11; http://www.childline.org.uk/bullying.html

Parentline Scotland: Freephone 0808 800 2222

Scottish Child Law Centre: Freephone 0800 317 500

Scottish Council for Research in Education http://www.scre.ac.uk/bully/index.html

Scottish Anti-Bullying Network: Tel. 0131 651 6100 ; www.antibullying.net

Legal references used in this section

Section 2 of the **Standards in Scotland's Schools etc. (Scotland) Act 2000**

Section 1 of the **Education (Scotland) Act 1980**

Reg 3(a) of the **Schools (Safety and Supervision of Pupils) (Scotland) Regulations 1990**

Ahmed v. City of Glasgow Council; 2000 GWD 26-1004

Montgomery v. Cumming (unreported, 17 December 1998, High Court of Justiciary)

Scott v. Lothian Regional Council 1999 RepLR 15; and Montgomery v. Cumming (unreported, 17 December 1998, High Court of Justiciary)

Skeen v. Tunnah 1970 SLT (Sh. Ct.) 66

CAREERS EDUCATION

The purpose of careers education is to provide those leaving education with information about

• what jobs or further training will be available to them,

• what further training or education is needed for certain jobs, and

• making applications for work, education and training.

There is only a requirement to make the careers service available to those in "relevant education" although it can be made available to those in other types of education, who are unemployed or who are already in work. *Relevant* education includes school education and some college courses (whether part or full time) but does not include higher education. Most higher education institutions will have their own careers service.

See also

Guidance

Legal references used in this section

Section 8 of the **Employment and Training Act 1973**, as amended by the **Trade Union Reform and Employment Rights Act 1993**

CHILDREN IN CARE

A large number of children and young people come to the attention of local authorities every year. This may be for a variety of reasons. For example, their parents may have difficulties in caring for them; they may be involved in offending or drug or alcohol misuse; or they may not be attending school. Most of these children receive a service from the local authority while they continue to live at home. Indeed, local authorities have an obligation to try to keep children at home with their parents or some other family member wherever possible. In some cases however, children cannot be cared for by their parents and may be taken into care by the local authority. The law says these children are "looked after" away from home by the local authority, and gives the local authority additional responsibilities towards them. Children can be looked after away from home in a number of different settings – some may stay with relatives or foster carers, others may stay in children's homes or residential schools. The local authority has an obligation to try to find the most appropriate placement for each child it looks after.

There are a number of ways that your child can be taken into care:

Voluntary care

Sometimes, parents ask for their children to be taken into local authority care. This can be for a variety of reasons. They may have to spend some time in hospital and have no one who can care for their child while they are away. They may be unable or unwilling to care for their child. There is no maximum or minimum period that a child can remain in care on a voluntary basis. Some children have a programme of "respite care" where they regularly spend a couple of nights every week or month in care on a planned basis.

Generally speaking, you have to sign a document agreeing to your child being taken into voluntary care. You can ask for your child to be returned to your care at any time, but you must give the local authority some notice of this. The amount of notice depends on the length of time your child has been in care. If the local authority has received a request for your child to be returned to you, but feels it would not be in your child's best interests to return home, it may take steps to have your child remain in care on a compulsory basis.

Very occasionally, children themselves may ask to be taken into local authority care.

Whenever children are in care on a voluntary basis, their parents retain all of their parental rights in relation to them. You must be consulted, and your views taken into account whenever decisions are being made, for example about a change of school or of placement.

Compulsory care

If the local authority believes it would be in your child's best interests to be in its care, but you do not agree, the authority can take steps to take your child into compulsory care. Authorisation for this can only be granted in very limited circumstances, for example if your child is at risk at home, or has committed offences or misused alcohol or drugs. In exceptional cases, your child may be taken into care as a result of a failure to attend school regularly.

In an emergency situation, e.g. where the local authority believes your child is at some immediate risk, it may apply to the court for a "child protection order." This authorises your child to remain in care for a short period until a children's hearing can be held to consider his/her case.

More commonly, authorisation for your child to be taken into care is given by a children's hearing. The children's hearing may issue a warrant which authorises your child to remain in care for periods of up to 22 days at a time, or may make a supervision requirement which can authorise your child to remain in care for up to one year.

If your child is in care on a compulsory basis, you still keep all of your parental rights in relation to education matters.

Assumption of parental rights

In very limited and exceptional cases, the local authority can take court action to assume parental rights over children who are in their care. If it is successful, the child's natural parents lose all of their parental responsibilities and rights to the local authority. This means that it is the local authority who makes decisions about the child's education, not the natural parents.

Children leaving care

If a child was "looked after" when he/she became of school leaving age, then the local authority has power to pay him/her a grant or make a contribution towards their accommodation and maintenance expenses while they are in education or employment, or are seeking employment.

See also

Children's hearings

Legal references used in this section

Section 30 of the **Children (Scotland) Act 1995**

CHILDREN'S HEARINGS

Children's hearings have to decide whether the children referred to them need any compulsory measures of supervision from the local authority. The hearing is made up of three volunteers – "panel members" – who receive specialist training before their appointment and throughout their service.

"Grounds for referral" to a children's hearing

Children can be referred to a children's hearing for one or more of the following reasons (or "grounds for referral"):

(a) they are beyond parental control;

(b) they are falling into bad associations or are exposed to moral danger;

(c) their parents are unable to offer them an appropriate level of care (it is worth noting that in the case of young children whose parents are failing to ensure they are attending school regularly without reasonable excuse, this may be viewed as a lack of parental care);

(d) they have been the victim of a "Schedule 1 offence" (e.g. physical or sexual abuse/assaults; neglect), or are living as part of the same household as another child who has been the victim of such an offence or as someone who has committed such an offence;

(e) they have failed to attend school regularly without reasonable excuse;

(f) they have committed an offence;

(g) they have misused solvents, alcohol or drugs

The Reporter to the Children's Panel

The Reporter to the Children's Panel is the person who decides whether your child should be referred to a children's hearing or not. Anyone who suspects that your child falls into one of the above categories can refer them to the Reporter. When the Reporter receives a referral on your child, they will begin an investigation into your child's circumstances, in order to establish:

- whether one of the grounds for referral exists;

- whether there is a need for support from the local authority in dealing with any difficulties which may be affecting your child; and

- whether this support is required on a compulsory (as opposed to voluntary) basis.

It is only if the answer to all three questions is 'yes' that the Reporter will refer your child to a children's hearing.

Social background reports

In order to arrive at his or her decision, the Reporter may request a variety of reports. In a large number of cases, the Reporter will request a report from your child's school initially, and may also ask a social worker to visit to provide a report on your child's home circumstances. This "social background report" will outline what local authority support your child and family may benefit from, and will provide an assessment of whether your child and family are willing and able to accept these on a voluntary basis. The Reporter will usually advise you that they are investigating your child's case. You and your child should give the Reporter your views about what should happen, to help the Reporter make the best decision for your child.

What information does the children's hearing receive?

The children's hearing will receive a copy of the grounds for referral, the school report, the social background report and any other reports which may be relevant to your child's case. If you or your child have given the Reporter your views, then the panel members will also receive copies of these.

The child's parents and main carers will receive a copy of all the papers which the panel members receive. Children however have no legal right to see the papers, although in practice, many social workers will go through the social background report with the child prior to the hearing.

Initial referral to the Children's Hearing

You and your child (if he/she is not presently subject to a "supervision requirement") will be sent a copy of the grounds for referral. These will tell you the legal basis for your child's referral to the hearing, and will include a statement of the facts the Reporter believes back up this legal basis.

At the beginning of the hearing, the chairperson will read out the grounds for referral, with the statement of facts, and will ask if you and your child understand and accept them.

The hearing cannot proceed to a full discussion about the case until you and your child accept the grounds for referral. If you or your child do not accept them, or if your child is too young to understand them, then the hearing must make a decision either to:

• refer your case to the sheriff court for proof, or to

• take no further action and dismiss the case on these grounds for referral.

Referral to the sheriff court for proof

If the hearing decides to refer your case to the sheriff court for proof, the Reporter will lead evidence from witnesses whom he believes will support the grounds for referral. You and your child can also call witnesses and lead evidence to show whether the grounds for referral should or should not be established by the sheriff.

At the end of the court case, the sheriff will decide whether the grounds for referral are established, based on the evidence and legal arguments he has heard. If he finds that the grounds have been established, he will refer the case back to another children's hearing. If he finds that the grounds for referral have not been established, he will take no further action and will dismiss the case on those grounds for referral.

Legal Aid is available for this part of the proceedings, and you should seek legal advice if you are unsure about the implications of the grounds for referral.

What happens at the children's hearing?

If the grounds for referral have been accepted or established, the children's hearing will go on to discuss your case in detail, with a view to deciding whether your child needs compulsory measures of supervision.

Usually, the social worker who compiled the social background report will be present. Your child's head teacher or guidance teacher may also be present. The hearing will discuss all of the issues fully with everyone who is present. They will ask you and your child for your views, and must take these into account before making their decision.

It can be worthwhile for you and your child to spend some time before the hearing thinking about and writing down what you would like to happen and why. This can be passed to the panel members before the hearing and can help make sure you don't miss anything out at the hearing. You should bear in mind that if you do this, then as well as being given to the panel members your written views will also be passed to certain other people attending the hearing, although not to your child.

At the end of the discussion, the hearing has to make a decision about whether the child needs compulsory measures of supervision. Occasionally, they may feel they do not have enough information at that time to make a proper decision, and they will continue the case to another day for further information. The children's hearing can make one of the following decisions:

To dismiss the case completely. They will do this if they feel that your child and family do not need any assistance from the local authority, or that if you do, it can be arranged voluntarily between you, and no compulsion is necessary.

To make the child subject to a supervision requirement. This would only be in cases where local authority assistance is required, but the hearing feels that this would not be effective unless it was made compulsory.

Each panel member must give their decision and the reasons for their decision in turn. The decision is reached by majority vote. After the hearing you will be sent out the reasons in writing.

What is a supervision requirement?

A supervision requirement is the legal document which says that the child is entitled and obliged to receive assistance from the local authority. It may have conditions attached which require the child to stay away from home (e.g. with relatives, in foster care, a children's home or residential school).

The vast majority of children who are subject to a supervision requirement remain at home, and it is only as a last resort that children will be removed from home. There may also be conditions attached relating to the child's regular attendance at school or nursery, or about who he/she can have contact with.

A supervision requirement cannot last for more than 12 months without being reviewed by a children's hearing. If you or your child would like a hearing to review the case earlier than this, you can ask the reporter to arrange a review hearing anytime after 3 months since the last hearing. The local authority can also ask for a review hearing at any time if they feel your child's case should be looked at again. In some cases the panel members may ask that a particular case is brought back to a hearing within the 12 months. They will say this when they are giving their decision and will specify when the hearing should take place.

What if I don't agree with the decision of the children's hearing?

If you or your child do not agree with the hearing's decision, you can appeal against it to the sheriff court. Your appeal must be lodged in court within 21 days of the hearing's decision. If you want to appeal against the decision, you should seek legal advice as soon as possible. Legal Aid is available for appeals to the sheriff court.

Where to find out more

"*Children's Hearings*" Factsheet 7 by the Scottish Office (available from the Scottish Executive).

Legal references used in this section

Sections 39-75 of the **Children (Scotland) Act 1995**

CHOICE OF SCHOOL (including placing requests)

In principle, your child can be educated in accordance with your wishes. This means that you may choose to educate your child at home, or to send him/her to an independent school for example. If you choose to send your child to a local authority school, then you have the right to choose *which* one to send your child to. However, this right is subject to a number of important restrictions.

Choosing a local authority school

The education authority decides on the "catchment areas" for each of its primary and secondary schools. These are largely based on the geographical area where you live, and in the case of secondary schools, certain primary schools may be "feeder" schools for particular secondaries. During the year before your child is due to start primary school or transfer to secondary school, the education authority will contact you telling you about your local school. It will also tell you about your right to make a "placing request" for your child to go to a different school instead, and will give you a date by which any placing request must be made. The education authority must place newspaper adverts telling parents about their right to make a placing request.

You have the right to request information on particular schools from the education authority. You can ask for this information from your own education authority, and also from other authorities whose schools you may be interested in. Remember that when making a major decision, you are obliged to consult your child, so you should discuss the options available with your child.

(If appropriate, you should read this section in conjunction with the **Special educational needs** section as there are special rules for children with a Record of Needs.)

Making a placing request

Education authorities must have guidelines for allocating places in schools if there are more placing requests than there are places available. If you want to make a placing request, you should ask the education authority to let you have a copy of its guidelines.

You can make a placing request at any time, and at any stage of your child's education. Most placing requests are made when a child is starting primary school or is transferring to secondary. You can make as many placing requests as you like and name as many schools as you like, although the education authority will only have to place your child in the first school named on your form.

Placing requests must be made in writing. Most education authorities have a standard form which they will send you. You do not have to give reasons why you would like your child to be placed in a particular school, although if the demand for places is high, then the more good reasons you give, (i.e. the more reasons why your child should be given priority) the better your chances of success. You should spend some time thinking about filling in this part of the form. If your child falls within one of the higher priority cases for placing in high demand schools, you should mention this. If there is a particular reason why this school would be more suitable for your child's abilities then you should include this too.

If you are making a placing request for a particular school at the start of the next session, you must receive a decision by 30 April. If you have applied at some other time of year, you must have a decision within 2 months of the date of your application. If you have not received a decision after 2 months, the education authority is deemed to have refused your application.

When can the education authority refuse a placing request?

If you make a placing request, the education authority must provide a place in the school you ask for, unless any of the following apply:

- Placing your child in the specified school would

  - Mean they had to employ another teacher;

  - Lead to significant expenditure to extend or alter the school accommodation or facilities;

  - Be seriously detrimental to your child's education;

  - Be likely to be seriously detrimental to order and discipline within the school;

  - Be likely to be seriously detrimental to the educational wellbeing of the pupils attending the school;

  - Make it necessary in future years for the authority to create an additional class or employ another teacher; or

  - Lead to the school capacity being exceeded.

- The education provided at that school is not suited to the age, ability or aptitude of your child;

- Your child had previously been excluded from that school;

- The school is a special school, but your child does not have the special needs it caters for;

- The school is a single sex school, and your child is not of the sex normally admitted there;

- Giving your child a place in the school would prevent the education authority keeping spaces there for children who may move into the area during the next year.

What can I do if my placing request is refused?

You can appeal against the refusal. Your appeal must be lodged within 28 days of the refusal (or the date your request was deemed to be refused). For more details about how to make an appeal, see the **Appeals** section.

One very important thing to bear in mind is that if you lodge an appeal against the refusal of a placing request, then you are not allowed to lodge another placing request appeal for the next 12 months. (This applies even if you withdraw your appeal before the committee hearing). You should therefore think carefully about lodging a placing request appeal; it may be a good idea to discuss it fully with a solicitor who has experience of education law.

Review of decisions

If a parent successfully appeals against the refusal of a placing request (whether at the appeal committee or the sheriff court stage) then the education authority must review all of the cases of children whose placing requests for the same stage of education at the same school were also refused. It must then notify the parents in writing whether on review, their child has now been granted a place at that school. These parents would then have 28 days from the date they received the review letter to lodge an appeal (provided they had not lodged an appeal within the previous 12 months).

See also

Appeals
Special educational needs

Where to find out more

"*Choosing a School – a guide for parents*" by the Scottish Executive.

Legal references used in this book

Section 28 of the **Education (Scotland) Act 1980**

CLASS SIZE AND STAFFING

Class sizes in Primary 1 to Primary 3

The maximum number of pupils who may be taught together in a class is set by law for Primary 1 to Primary 3 classes (as from 1 August 2001) at thirty pupils. This limit applies during the course of "ordinary teaching sessions", that is it does not include school assemblies or other similar activities. Larger classes are permitted, as long as there are no more than 30 pupils for every qualified teacher.

There are exceptions to these rules where, during the first school year:

• a child moves into the catchment area of a school; or

• is placed there after a successful appeal against a refused placing request; or

• has the school named within a Record of Needs; or

• where there has been an error on the part of the education authority.

The limit does not affect the occasional teaching of children with special educational needs within a mainstream class, where those children are normally educated at a special school or at a specialist unit within the school.

Other class sizes in primary and secondary schools

The maximum number of pupils for other classes in primary and secondary schools is set by the education authority in line with the terms of the contracts with their teachers.

The maximum number of pupils should not normally be more than:

33 pupils in Primary 4 – 7 and Secondary 1 & 2;
30 pupils in Secondary 3 – 6 ; and
20 pupils in practical classes at secondary school (such as home economics, science, and technical classes).

Teachers may be asked to teach larger classes than these in certain circumstances (e.g. to cover for staff absences). They may not refuse to do so without good reason.

There are, however, *absolute* maximum limits which may not be exceeded and above which teachers may refuse to teach under any circumstances:

39 pupils in Primary 4 – 7 and Secondary 1 & 2; and
34 pupils in Secondary 3 & 4.

The education authority also has to make sure that there are not too many pupils in one classroom at a time, taking into consideration things like: the school building regulations, the space available, any equipment in the classroom, the type of classes taught there, and any health and safety considerations. The education authority must keep a record of room sizes and the number of pupils they can hold, and you may ask to view these.

Composite classes

Pupils from different age groups may sometimes be taught together in one "composite" class. Composite classes should be smaller than classes otherwise would be. Recommendations state that they should be no more than 25.

Official guidelines state that composite classes, where possible, should **not**:

• have pupils from more than two different age groups, which should be consecutive (e.g. P4/5, but not P4/5/6, nor P3/5);

• be set up just for convenience without first considering any possible alternatives; nor

- be formed or regrouped after the school year has started (other than for educational reasons).

School Staffing

The number of teaching staff is decided by the education authority, taking into account the numbers recommended by the Scottish Executive.

Official guidance covers the basic number of teachers in any particular primary school. It is based on the number of pupils attending. The recommended number goes from:

- one teacher for schools with a roll of one to nineteen,

- up to 25 teachers for schools with a roll of 632 to 658.

In secondary schools, the staff numbers are worked out according to the number of pupils taking different courses and subjects there, the number of teaching periods, "non-teaching" time and other factors.

Additional funds to provide for extra teachers above the basic complement may be available to schools:

- which are difficult to run because of small or changing pupil numbers;

- with a lot of pupils from socially-disadvantaged areas who need extra tuition; or

- at which staff are away training or otherwise out of the classroom.

See also

Special educational needs

Legal references used in this section

Education (Lower Primary Class Sizes) (Scotland) Regulations 1999

Scottish Office Education Department **Circular 14; December 1978, No. 1029**

Scheme of Salaries and Conditions of Teaching Staff in School Education. 10.12.1 & 10.12.2

Reg 8(1) & (2) of the **Schools General (Scotland) Regulations 1975**

"Scheme of Conditions of Service" Scottish Joint Negotiating Committee for Teaching Staff in School Education; **STC/19 (Composite Class Guidelines)**

CLOTHING AND SCHOOL UNIFORM

Clothing

What help with clothing should be available?

The law says that local authorities must provide any grants that they consider necessary to help with costs of clothing for pupils attending schools in their area. Each has its own scheme for clothing grants, and you should contact your child's school for more information on the scheme operating in your area.

The education authority must provide clothing (not necessarily free of charge) for any child whose inadequate or unsuitable clothes mean that he/she is unable to take full advantage of his/her education. It also has wide-ranging powers to provide clothing in a variety of circumstances. In practice, these powers are almost always exercised by way of a clothing grant scheme. However, the education authority must consider other requests made for clothing to be provided, even if they do not come within the scheme.

How much assistance is there?

The amount of the grant is decided by the education authority and will depend on your income and other circumstances – most education authorities provide some financial assistance if you are in receipt of Income Support or Working Families' Tax Credit. It is up to you to apply for a clothing grant. It should cover some or all of the costs of any clothes and shoes required to enable your child to attend school, and any other special items of clothing required (e.g. PE kit) which are not provided by the school.

A clothing grant may be provided in cash but is more often provided by way of vouchers.

Uniform

Does my child have to wear school uniform?

The law is not specific on the question of school uniform. Nothing in the law says that your child has to wear a school uniform. In practice, the rules about school uniform are left for the education authority or the school to decide. This can lead to considerable variation in the amount of freedom given to pupils on the types of clothes they can wear.

Schools almost always have rules or guidelines on the types of clothes allowed or preferred. This may include some common-sense rules which are imposed for health or safety reasons, for example:

* specialist sportswear may be required for certain activities (swimming caps, football boots etc.);

* loose clothing and dangling earrings may be forbidden in technical subjects using machinery or in PE where there may be a risk of injury.

Other rules on clothing or uniform may be to allow the school to promote a certain image or to improve the school ethos or discipline.

Where there is a school board, the head teacher must provide it with a copy of the school's policy on school uniform and let it know about any future changes to the policy.

Written information on clothing and uniform must also be made available to parents. Each school must provide information on its policy on clothing and uniform, including the approximate cost of each item of required uniform. The education authority must provide written information on its general policy on wearing school uniform.

Can my child be excluded for not wearing the uniform?

Your child could face exclusion from school for breaking school rules on suitable dress. However, this would only be lawful where either:

* you have prevented your child from wearing the correct clothes, or

* your child's refusal is likely to cause a serious disciplinary or academic problem within the school.

What about human rights?

The European Commission of Human Rights has decided that it is not a breach of human rights to insist on school uniform being worn, although it had previously decided that it was a breach of a prisoner's human rights to be made to wear a uniform! This decision was based largely on the fact that the requirement only lasted during school hours, and therefore was not so serious as to constitute a breach of the Convention.

Discrimination

School rules on uniform must not have a disproportionate effect on one gender or race, nor impose a substantial disadvantage for children with disabilities (as of September 2002). Rules that do are unlawful, unless justified on objective grounds. For example, a rule that girl pupils may not wear trousers might be indirect discrimination on the grounds of race, as it would affect a greater proportion of Muslim pupils.

See also

Equal opportunities
Exclusion from school

Legal references used in this section

Section 11; 54; 55 and 56 of the **Education (Scotland) Act 1980**, as amended

Section 10(2)(c) of the **School Boards (Scotland) Act 1988**

Education (School and Placing Information) (Scotland) Regulations 1982

See Shaw v. Strathclyde Regional Council 1988 SLT 313

Stevens v. UK, 3 March 1986 (unreported)

McFeeley v. UK, Application No. 8317/78, D.R. 20 p. 44; X. v. UK, Application No. 8231/78, D.R. 28 p. 5

COMPLAINTS

What to do when something goes wrong

Parents and children are free to complain to various bodies or individuals when they are dissatisfied with something to do with their education. You should first try to get a problem or difficulty sorted out informally. The steps below should help you make sure that a problem or difficulty is presented in the right way to the right people.

Before making a complaint, you should first ask yourself:

Is your complaint justified? Do you have reliable evidence to back up your claim? Talk to everybody concerned to try to discover the facts, or take it to a higher level until you do so. You should be cautious about airing your complaints in public as you could find yourself being accused of defamation (slander).

Who is the best person to complain to? Often this will be the head teacher or another senior member of staff at the school concerned, but there may be circumstances in which it is appropriate to take your complaint to:

• A member of your school board or parents' group

• The education authority

• An elected representative

• The Commissioner for Local Administration (commonly known as the Local Government Ombudsman)

• The Scottish Ministers.

Certain official bodies also deal with complaints about:

- Professional conduct of teachers – General Teaching Council for Scotland;

- Racial discrimination – Commission for Racial Equality;

- Sex discrimination – Equal Opportunities Commission;

- Disability discrimination – Disability Rights Commission.

You should note, too, that certain legal procedures exist for hearing appeals from parents against a choice of school or exclusion from school. Some voluntary organisations may also agree to help you with your complaint. A list of these appears at the end of the book.

Next you should consider:

How should your complaint be presented? The best way to start may be by talking to the people concerned, usually the head teacher or another senior staff member. You may wish to confirm what was said in writing to them afterwards. Complaints should be put in writing if informal approaches have failed, and copies should be kept of all correspondence. You should be polite, but firm and insistent on getting an answer. You may wish somebody to represent you, such as a friend, advice worker, representative from a parents' group, or a solicitor.

Complaints to the head teacher

It is advisable to take any complaints you have about a school to the head teacher or another member of staff to start with. If this is unsuccessful or the complaint is about the head teacher, you may wish to approach one of the other bodies mentioned below. The head teacher may wish to make some enquiries into your complaint and you should allow a reasonable time for this in waiting for an answer.

Complaints to the school board or PTA/PA

Complaints of a non-personal kind, for example about a shortage of school textbooks or about courses taught at the school, may be worth taking to your school board or PTA/PA, if your school has one. They may be able to put some pressure on the school or education authority to see what can be done. Complaints about policy matters can be drawn to the attention of national parents' organisations which might be interested in bringing them to the attention of central or local government. These are listed at the end of the book.

Complaints to the education authority

Complaints which the school is unable or unwilling to deal with satisfactorily, should be addressed to the director of education or divisional education officer for your area. The education authority may have to make enquiries of its own, so it may be some time before you receive a detailed answer.

Complaints to elected representatives

You can write to or arrange to see your local councillor or MSP to take up a complaint about a school or education service in general. The best time to do this is probably after you have already complained to the school or education authority without a satisfactory outcome. Your elected representative is not legally obliged to deal with your complaint, but it is likely that he/she may agree to make enquiries on your behalf.

Complaints to the Scottish Ministers

You can make a complaint to the Scottish Ministers if you think an education authority has failed to carry out its legal duties. You should take advice before doing so.

The Scottish Ministers can conduct a local enquiry into your complaint, but they do not have to. They must give the education authority the opportunity to reply to your complaint. If they are satisfied that the authority is at fault, they can order it to carry out its duty or take whatever measures are considered necessary. If the authority refuses to act within the time limit given, the matter may be referred to the Court of Session to force it to carry out its legal duty.

Complaints to the Local Government Ombudsman

You can complain to the Local Government Ombudsman (Commissioner for Local Administration in Scotland) if you believe you have been unjustly treated by the education authority as a result of bad administration. The Ombudsman will, if necessary, look into your complaint and issue a report saying whether or not there has been "maladministration" and if so what should be done. Although the recommendations are not legally binding, in the great majority of cases local authorities accept and act upon the findings. Maladministration may occur where:

A rule has been unfairly or inefficiently applied or where the rule itself has caused the problem and could be improved.

A procedure has not been correctly followed.

Unreasonable delay or inefficiency has occurred in dealing with something.

Misleading or incorrect advice or information has been given, whether verbally or in writing.

There has been a failure to keep somebody properly informed about a decision or proposal.

Somebody has been treated with lack of proper consideration or respect.

You must make sure that you have already used the education authority's own complaints procedures first. Otherwise the Ombudsman cannot take up your complaint, except where it would be unreasonable to expect you to have done so.

A copy of the Ombudsman's report must be issued to you and copies must be available at the local authority's offices for any member of the public to look at.

See also

Advice and assistance
Appeals
Legal action

Section 70 of the **Education (Scotland) Act 1980**

Sections 10 and 11 of the **Teaching Council (Scotland) Act 1965**

CONSULTING CHILDREN

Scots law views children very much as individuals with rights, and this is complemented by legal obligations to consult children and seek their views. However, while there is generally an obligation to *have regard* to the views of children, there is no absolute obligation to follow them. Generally speaking, the requirement to seek a child's views depends on the age and level of maturity of the individual child, although a child of 12 is presumed to be of sufficient age and maturity to form a view on matters. (Children under 12 may be of sufficient age and maturity to form a view, but this will depend on the individual child and the complexity of the matter in hand).

Parents

Parents are required by law to seek their child's views (and to have regard to those views) when making a major decision involving the fulfilment of parental responsibilities or the exercise of parental rights. Decisions about your child's education, such as the choice of school, or home education are examples of the types of decisions where you should seek and take into account your child's views.

Local authorities

The level of the local authority's duty to consult children depends to an extent on whether the child is "looked after" by it. (A child is "looked after" if he/she is in local authority care, whether on a compulsory or voluntary basis, or if he/she is subject to a supervision requirement issued by a children's hearing).

The education authority has a duty to make sure the education provided to each pupil is directed towards the development of the individual pupil's talents and abilities. When deciding how best to fulfil this duty, the education authority must seek the views of the individual pupil(s). This may be particularly relevant where the education authority is considering whether to educate a child outwith mainstream schooling, or is making decisions about the range of subjects offered in a particular school.

There is now a duty on education authorities to issue an "annual statement of education improvement objectives" setting out their objectives for improving standards in school education in their areas. The education authority must give children in its area an opportunity to give their views on what the statement should include. Each school must also issue an annual "school development plan" setting out how it plans to improve the quality of education within the school. The pupils attending the school must be given the opportunity to make their views known on what should be in the development plan.

If a child is "looked after" by the local authority, then the local authority must seek (and have regard to) their views when making *any* decision about the child (compare this with the parent's duty to consult only when it's a *major* decision).

Children's hearings

When making any decision, children's hearings must give your child an opportunity to express their views and have regard to these views. Your child's views on education may be particularly relevant where they are considering moving him/her to a foster home which may lead to a change of school, or are considering a requirement that he/she should stay at a residential school.

Courts

In relation to education matters, courts are only really required to take into account your child's views when they are deciding whether to substitute their decision for that of the children's hearing in the event of a successful appeal.

See also

Children in care
Children's hearings
Children's rights

Where to find out more

"*Giving Children a Voice - what next? a study from one primary school*" Spotlights no. 65 by the Scottish Council for Research in Education (1997).

Legal references used in this section

Section 2; 5 and 6 of the **Standards in Scotland's Schools etc. (Scotland) Act 2000**

CONSULTING PARENTS

You have a right to be consulted by the education authority before it goes ahead with certain decisions about the education provision in your area. These include:

School closure (or partial school closure)

If the education authority proposes to close your school or to stop providing a "stage of education" (a year stage or all the school's nursery classes) at the school, it must first conduct a period of consultation. This involves consulting the parents of every pupil in the school or stage and of every pupil who is expected to be at the school or in the stage in the next two years. It also has to consult the school board (if there is one) and the appropriate church or other body if it is a denominational school. Similar consultation is required to change a single-sex school into a "co-ed" school.

Moving the location of a school

Where the education authority proposes to change the site of your school, it must first conduct a period of consultation. This involves consulting the parents of every pupil in the school or expected to be at the school in the next two years. It also has to consult the school board (if there is one) and the appropriate church or other body if it is a denominational school.

Opening a new school

Where the education authority proposes to open a new school, it must consult the parents of every pupil who will have to move to the school and of every pupil who would be expected to start attending the school in the next two years.

Similar consultation is required to alter the catchment area of a school.

The Standards in Scotland's Schools etc. (Scotland) Act 2000 includes many provisions to make sure that you are consulted on key issues at both school and education authority level. For example:

Annual statement of education improvement objectives

Each year the education authority must prepare and publish a statement setting its objectives for improving education, in line with the current national priorities in education and performance indicators (as defined by the Scottish Ministers). It must consult with parents' groups (among others) in preparing the statement. The statement must include details of how the education authority will try to involve parents in promoting the education of their children. An annual report on its success (or otherwise) in meeting these objectives must also be prepared.

School Development Plan

Each year the education authority must prepare, for each of its schools, a school development plan. The development plan sets objectives for each school based on the annual statement of education improvement objectives. The development plan must be prepared after consultation with (among others) the school board, and any parents' groups for that school. Again an annual report must be prepared to show what has been done to put the plan into practice within the school.

Parents of pupils at the school are entitled to free access to the plan and the report on request (and to a free copy of their summaries).

Review of school performance

The education authority must, from time to time, assess the quality of each school's education against its own measures and standards for judging performance. Where a school fails to meet the standards, the education authority must take action to put right the problem(s).

When deciding the measures and standards of performance, the education authority must consult with parents' groups (among others). The measures and standards must be published.

Sex education

Although there is no statutory requirement to consult in relation to sex education, government guidance states that schools should consult parents and carers when developing their sex education programmes, and parents and carers should have the opportunity to examine the materials which will be used, in advance.

How does the education authority consult?

The education authority will notify you by sending you the proposals, and allowing 28 days for representations or comments to be received in response. It may also give notice of any meeting to be held for parents to discuss the proposals. The notification can be posted or sent home with your child, but it must reach all parents (including guardians and anyone else with parental responsibility for the pupil). For parents of children not yet at school, notification may have to be by advertisement in a local newspaper.

A school board or denominational body must receive the full details of the proposal and, again, have 28 days to respond.

The education authority must take into account all representations it receives about a particular proposal. It must do so with the general principle that children are to be educated in accordance with the wishes of their parents, as far as this is compatible with suitable instruction and training and avoids unreasonable public expenditure. Failure to take these matters into account may lead to the possibility of a decision being overturned by judicial review.

See also

Parent-teacher and parents' associations
Information for parents
Legal action
School boards
School closures and changes

Legal references used in this section

Sections 4; 5(1); 5(2)(a); 5(4); 5(6); 6(1); 6(2); 6(4); 6(5); 7(1); 7(2) of the **Standards in Scotland's Schools etc. (Scotland) Act 2000**

Scottish Executive **Circular 2/2001**, issued in terms of section 56 of the Standards in Scotland's Schools etc. (Scotland) Act 2000

Education (Publication and Consultation etc) (Scotland) Regulations 1981

See Harvey v. Strathclyde Regional Council 1989 SLT 612

CURRICULUM (what is taught)

"Curriculum" is the word used to describe what is taught to your child. It refers to the full range of subjects that are studied at a school.

What is taught at school

By law there are only three subjects which must be taught by schools:

• Religious education;

• Gaelic in Gaelic speaking areas; and

• Physical education, social and recreational activities.

Beyond this, the Scottish Executive issues guidelines on the curriculum, which are followed to a greater or lesser extent by education authorities. Whether the curriculum guidelines are closely adhered to or not, the education authority has a duty to provide your child with an adequate and efficient education suitable to his/her age, aptitude and ability. It must also be directed to the development of the personality, talents and mental and physical abilities to his/her fullest potential. The education authority and head teachers share responsibility for the management and delivery of the curriculum. In the case of independent schools, it is the governors (or other managing body) and the head teacher.

The 5 to 14 curriculum

These guidelines cover primary school education and the first stages of secondary school education. The guidelines try to make sure that the curriculum is:

- Broad: covering a wide range of subject areas;

- Balanced: giving due attention to each area;

- Coherent: building on what pupils have already learned; and

- Progressive: providing challenging but attainable targets for all pupils.

Primary Education

The 5 to 14 curriculum covers five broad subject areas which are taught at primary school level:

- Language: reading, writing, discussion, possibly Gaelic or other languages;

- Mathematics: number, shape, etc.;

- Expressive arts: art, craft, music, physical education, drama;

- Environmental studies: geography, history, nature study, science etc.; and

- Religious and moral education.

Secondary Education

The five areas listed above become, in the first two years of secondary school, eight broader areas of study:

- Language and Communication: including English (language and literature) and foreign languages;

- Mathematical Studies and Applications;

- Creative and Aesthetic Activities: including art, drama and music;

- Scientific Studies and Applications;

- Technological Activities and Applications;

- Social and Environmental Studies; including geography, history, modern studies etc.

- Physical Education; and

- Religious and Moral Education

Assessment

Subject areas are assessed at six levels, starting at level A in primary one and working through to level E which should be attained by second year at secondary school. A level F is also available to continue to challenge pupils who may reach level E before then. Pupils are allowed to progress through the levels at their own pace, being regularly assessed by their teacher. For Maths and English, there are compulsory national tests to assess the level of attainment.

Beyond 5 to 14

Beyond the 5 to 14 age range, there are no curriculum guidelines. It is expected that most pupils will take courses leading to the award of standard grades and / or other certificates.

See also

Bilingual education (including Gaelic)
Examinations and assessment
Religious education and observance

Where to find out more

"The Structure and Balance of the Curriculum: 5-14 National Guidelines" by Learning and Teaching Scotland (2000).

"Higher Still – new courses and qualifications in Scotland from August 1999" by the Scottish Office (1998). Available from the Scottish Executive.

"It all adds up: helping your children with numeracy" by the Scottish Executive (2000).

"Which way now? Study decisions at 14" by the Scottish Executive (2001).

"Higher Still: a simple guide for parents" by the Scottish Parent Teacher Council.

"Scottish Certificate of Education Standard Grade. Factsheet 5" by the Scottish Office (1996). Available from the Scottish Executive.

"Teachers' and Pupils' days in the primary classroom" by the Scottish Council for Research in Education (1999)

Legal references used in this section

Section 2(1) of the **Standards in Scotland's Schools etc. (Scotland) Act 2000**

Sections 1 and 8 of the **Education (Scotland) Act 1980**

DENOMINATIONAL SCHOOLS

Many pupils in Scotland go to schools which are associated with a religious denomination. Most are Roman Catholic schools, managed by the education authority, though there are others, including non-Christian schools (such as Jewish; Sikh; or Islamic). Although primarily intended for children of parents belonging to the denomination in question, they must also be open to other children. Any church or other religious body can ask the education authority to open a denominational school. The education authority does not have to do this, although it may decide to if there is likely to be sufficient demand. Religious bodies can also establish their own, independent schools.

The right to respect for a parent's religious convictions in providing education does not mean that a parent can insist on a school being provided, or on a place for their child at a denominational school.

Management of denominational schools

Denominational schools are subject to all the same legal requirements as other local authority schools. Even the rules for religious education and observance are the same. There are also additional rules which apply only to denominational schools. At a denominational school:

- Teachers appointed must have their religious beliefs and character approved by the religious body;

- The amount of religious education and observance cannot be less than is customary for schools of that type;

- The school must allow for religious examinations to be held;

- An unpaid supervisor of religious instruction (e.g. a priest, rabbi or imam) approved by the religious body must report to the education authority on the efficiency of religious education provided. The supervisor may attend the school any time religious instruction is to be provided.

Complaints about whether the school is complying with these obligations may be dealt with by the Scottish Ministers, if they are asked to look into the matter.

The education authority remains responsible for deciding on the curriculum (what is to be taught) at denominational schools, in consultation with the religious body.

Attendance

Your child cannot be refused admission on the grounds of their or your religious affiliations. Nor can a religious body insist that your child attend a certain school.

Religious education and observance

The rules are exactly the same as for other schools, including your right to withdraw your child from religious education or observance. If your child is a boarder, he/she has the right to be allowed time outside school hours to practice your (or their) religion, even if this is different from the school's.

School transport

Free school transport must be provided in accordance with the statutory rules if the education authority offers your child a place at a denominational school. However, where the school placement is as a result of a placing request, the education authority has no obligation to provide free transport.

See also

Equal opportunities
Religious education and observance
Transport

Legal references used in this section

Article 2, Protocol 1, Schedule 1 of the **Human Rights Act 1998**

Sections 9, 10 and 70 of the **Education (Scotland) Act 1980**

Belgian Linguistic Case (No 2) (1979-80) 1EHRR 252

DEVOLVED SCHOOL MANAGEMENT

While in the majority of cases, it is the education authority (rather than the school itself) that has legal duties towards pupils, many of the day to day tasks and responsibilities are carried out by the head teachers and senior management teams of the schools, as part of the education authority. Education authorities must have a scheme for delegating responsibility for preparing school development plans to the head teachers of each school. This scheme can (but does not have to) delegate other management responsibilities to the head teacher. This puts the practice of "devolved school management" on a statutory footing.

The thinking behind devolved school management is to give to those who know the school best more involvement in and responsibility for decision making.

Schools are given a budget to cover, for example, salaries, costs of books and other teaching materials, costs of furniture, fixtures and fittings, and costs of other supplies and services. The head teacher, in consultation with other teachers in the school and with the school board, then decides how to allocate the school's budget. Parents do not have to be formally consulted. However, if parents feel additional expenditure is needed in a particular area, then they are free to raise this with the head teacher. If parents remain unhappy with the way the school budget is being spent, then they can raise this with the education authority.

Under a scheme of devolved school management, head teachers can also be given increased responsibility for staff recruitment.

Where to find out more

"A Simple Outline of Devolved School Management" by the Scottish Parent Teacher Council.

Legal references used in this section

Section 8 of the **Standards in Scotland's Schools etc. (Scotland) Act 2000**

DISCIPLINE AND PUNISHMENT

Part of a school's function is to encourage in pupils the development of responsible social attitudes and relationships, consideration for others, and good manners. Schools have a duty not to allow serious disruption to the educational well being of their pupils. They have duties relating to the safety and supervision of their pupils as well as duties (as employers) to their staff. They therefore have a legitimate interest in maintaining good order and asking you to comply with school rules.

Accordingly, schools may exercise or impose reasonable disciplinary measures as part of a behaviour management policy.

Promoting Positive Behaviour

Recent thinking about discipline has focused on promoting positive behaviour in the classroom, and on positive reinforcement as the method for achieving this. Considerable success has been achieved in avoiding the need to resort to traditional disciplinary measures (although these are not abandoned and are used where necessary).

Key features of positive reinforcement / promoting positive behaviour are:

• "Good" behaviour is behaviour which allows effective learning to take place;

• Developing pupils' behaviour is best and most effective by way of positive reinforcement (involving behavioural targets and rewarding positive behaviour);

• Pupils should take responsibility for their own behaviour and have the capacity to alter negative behavioural habits;

- Positive peer pressure can encourage changes in negative behaviour as part of a class-wide approach; and

- Discipline should not be confrontational because this undermines the promotion of positive behaviour by weakening the teacher / pupil relationship.

Restrictions on the use of discipline

There are limits to the punishment schools can use, as well as to the circumstances in which they can punish pupils. You may be able to make a legal challenge if the school takes disciplinary action that breaks these limits. For example:

Corporal (or physical) punishment is now unlawful in all schools, including independent schools, and may result in criminal charges if used. However this does not include anything done to stop immediate danger to someone's personal safety or their property.

Disciplinary measures should not be unreasonable, should not be excessive, and should be in line with any policy, guidelines or procedures laid down by the school or education authority. The policies on discipline should be available to parents.

The school must make sure that any punishment does not amount to unlawful discrimination, for example where negative behaviour is caused by a pupil's disability.

The school should consider your religious and/or philosophical convictions before it takes any disciplinary action.

Disciplinary measures must not be imposed if it would amount to inhuman or degrading treatment.

Detention must be very carefully managed, and your and/or your child's permission will be needed before it is used. Failure to obtain permission might make the detention unlawful, which would be a serious human rights (and possibly criminal law) matter. Unlawful deprivation of liberty would also justify a compensation claim under the common law.

Where a disciplinary measure could be seen as a violation of your child's human rights, there must be some method of appeal available to allow you to reverse the decision.

See also

Equal opportunities
Legal action
Safety and supervision
School rules

Legal references used in this section

Section 48A of the Education (Scotland) Act 1980; Section 16 of the **Standards in Scotland's Schools etc. (Scotland) Act 2000**

Sched I, Part I, Art 3 & Art 5; and Sched I, Part II, Prot 1, Art 2 of the **Human Rights Act 1998**

Sched I, Part II(k) & III(w) of the **Education (School and Placing Information) (Scotland) Regulations 1982**

Reg 11 of the **Schools General (Scotland) Regulations 1975**

Valsamis v. Greece (1996) 24 EHRR 294

Warwick v. United Kingdom (1986) 60 DR 5

Campbell and Cosans v. United Kingdom (1982) 4 EHRR 293

Article 13 of the European Convention on Human Rights

EDUCATION AUTHORITIES

There are 32 local authorities throughout Scotland. Local authorities have duties covering a whole host of public matters, including education. Each local authority consists of its elected members – councillors – and its employees who have the task of putting into practice the council's policies and carrying out its various duties. For the purposes of the education legislation, each local authority is called an education authority.

Education committees

The education authority must set up an education committee, which deals with policy issues in relation to education. The committee will be made up of councillors, teachers, representatives of religious bodies and may also include parent or pupil representatives. The education committee may also set up sub-committees to deal with specific issues. The meetings of the education committee and sub-committees are open to the public. Copies of the agendas for the meetings, reports to be considered and the minutes of previous meetings should be made available to you. There are specific matters which the education committee is entitled by law to keep confidential and is allowed to refuse public access to meetings and reports.

The Director of Education

Each local authority will have a number of departments devoted to the different areas of work it is responsible for. One of these departments, headed by the Director of Education, will deal with the local authority's duties in relation to education.

What must education authorities do?

The law says that there are some things an education authority must do. For example:

• Make sure there is "adequate and efficient" provision of school and further education in its area;

• Make sure the education provided to each child at its schools is directed towards the development of the personality, talents and mental and physical abilities of that child to their fullest potential;

• Provide for special educational needs;

• Provide boarding accommodation where necessary;

• Provide books, stationery, etc;

• Consult with parents about school closures, etc.;

• Provide parents with information about schools;

• Provide a psychological service;

• Make sure pupils are adequately supervised;

• Provide adequate facilities for social, cultural and recreative activities for school pupils;

• Provide adequate facilities for physical education and training for school pupils;

If the law says an education authority has a duty to do something then it must carry out its duty. It would not be allowed to refuse to carry out a duty because it doesn't have enough money, although if there are a number of ways of carrying out the duty, it can choose how to do so.

What other things can the education authority do?

Additionally, the law gives education authorities powers to do certain things. These are things they do not have to do if they do not want to or do not have enough money. Examples of an education authority's powers include:

- Provide nursery schools/classes;

- Provide school meals and milk;

- Authorise medical examination of pupils in the interests of cleanliness;

- Provide school library facilities;

- Establish and maintain swimming pools, sports centres, youth and community centres and clubs

Can the education authority do whatever it wants to?

If an education authority has neither the *duty* nor the *power* to do something, it is not allowed to do it. This means that you cannot insist that it does something it is not allowed to do. It also means that if the education authority does something it is not authorised to do, and this affects you or your child, then you may be able to take legal action to stop the authority from doing it.

Complaints

If you think your education authority is not carrying out its legal duties or has done something it is not authorised to do, you should attempt to address this through the education authority's own internal complaints procedures. If that fails, you may be able to refer the matter to the Scottish Ministers or to the Local Government Ombudsman. You can of course raise an action in the courts either in your own name or your child's.

See also

Complaints
Legal action

EMPLOYMENT OF SCHOOLCHILDREN

Schoolchildren aged 14 and over are allowed to take on part-time work, subject to a number of limitations on the times and hours worked and the type of work involved. Children under 14 can be employed by their parents on an occasional basis to do light agricultural or horticultural work.

These are the statutory limitations on the employment of schoolchildren:

> No child of school age is allowed to work before 7am or after 7pm on any day or for more than 2 hours on a school day or a Sunday.

> 15 year olds are allowed to work 8 hours on any day which is not a school day or a Sunday, while 14 year olds are only allowed to work 5 hours on these days, subject to an overall limit of 35 hours per week for 15 year olds and 25 hours per week for 14 year olds.

> Children of school age are not allowed to work more than 4 hours in a day without having a break of one hour, and must have a period of at least 2 weeks in a year when they are not either working or at school.

An employer who breaks these restrictions can be prosecuted. You may be asked for information about your child's employment, and a deliberate failure to provide accurate information can also lead to your prosecution.

In addition to these statutory limitations on the employment of schoolchildren, there may be additional local bye-laws in your area. You should check with your local authority what these are. It is important to remember that the statutory limitations cover both paid and voluntary work. Local bye-laws cover the restrictions on children being employed in street trading.

Public performances

Children can take part in public performances (e.g. stage, television, film) and rehearsals as long as a licence is granted by their education authority. (No licence is needed for school or amateur productions). There is however an absolute prohibition on children of school age taking part in performances which endanger their life or limb (including acrobatic performances). Children aged 12 or over can be *trained* to take part in dangerous performances, so long as the person training them has obtained a licence.

Work experience

During your child's final year at school he/she will normally undertake a period of work experience. This usually lasts for about a week, but can last longer by arrangement between the education authority and "employer". The legal limitations on the *time* or *hours* worked will not apply during this period of work experience, although the limitations on the *type* of work will still apply. Your child will not be paid for the work he/she does during the work experience placement, although additional travelling expenses will be covered. Children undergoing work experience will not be covered by employer's liability or industrial injury protections (because the child is not "in employment"), but the education authority is expected to take out adequate insurance for accidents or injuries during the work experience period.

Once a child reaches school leaving age, the above restrictions no longer apply, even if he/she is still attending school. There are restrictions on the type of work under 18's are allowed to do, and these will obviously apply until the child is 18.

Legal references used in this section

Sections 28-38 of the **Children and Young Persons (Scotland) Act 1937**, as amended.

Employment of Children Act 1973

Section 123 **of the Education (Scotland) Act 1980**

EQUAL OPPORTUNITIES
(including sex, race and disability discrimination)

Each year the education authority must publish its education improvement objectives, which must include a statement of how it will improve equal opportunities and meet equal opportunities requirements.

In Scots Law there are three forms of discrimination that are unlawful. These are discrimination on the grounds of:

• race (race, colour, nationality, citizenship, ethnic or national origin);

• sex (gender or marital status); and

• disability.

Race Discrimination

Race discrimination can occur in two ways:

Directly – treating a person, on "racial grounds", less favourably than other people in similar circumstances;

Indirectly – where a rule or condition which applies to everyone, actually affects one "racial group" a lot more than others, to their detriment, <u>and</u> this cannot be justified by other (lawful) reasons.

"Racial grounds" means on the grounds of colour, race, nationality or ethnic or national origins. "Racial group" means a group of people defined by reference to their colour, race, nationality or ethnic or national origins. You may belong to more than one racial group.

Direct discrimination can take many forms. In a school setting this might include racist insults or comments, racially motivated harassment, or more subtle differences in marking or treatment. The education authority and the school must take reasonable steps to protect your child from unlawful discrimination at school. If they do not, then the education authority may be held responsible for the discriminatory actions of another pupil or a visitor to the school.

Indirect discrimination can sometimes be justified by other (lawful) reasons. In schools, there should be an educational justification for most (or all) differences of this type. Any potential justification must outweigh the disadvantage suffered by the people affected.

For example, a rule banning any headwear in school uniform was indirect discrimination, because it affects those who are required to wear turbans for cultural reasons. However, it would not be discrimination to ban Sikh ceremonial daggers, nor Scottish dirks, because this is justifiable on the grounds of safety.

It is unlawful for schools to discriminate on the grounds of race in any of the following:

• Decisions or policies on admission;

• Access to educational benefits, grants, bursaries, facilities, or other services;

• School meals, transport or uniform;

• Exclusions;

or by subjecting pupils to any other disadvantage.

In general, the education authority must not discriminate when carrying out any of its education functions and must make sure that facilities for education and any ancillary benefits are provided without race discrimination.

By law, local authorities have due regard to the need to eliminate unlawful race discrimination and promote equal opportunities and good relations between people of different races. The

Scottish Ministers will shortly have powers to instruct local authorities on how they should do this.

Exclusions

It is unlawful to racially discriminate when excluding a pupil. Schools should take care that the same rules are applied to all pupils and that these do not unfairly disadvantage one group.

There would be indirect discrimination if a school's decisions about exclusions affected proportionally more from one racial group and this could not be justified on educational grounds.

Assessment

It is direct discrimination if your child is given lower marks on racial grounds. This can come from overt prejudice, or unconscious assumptions about the relative abilities and characteristics of different racial groups.

Indirect discrimination might occur where assessment criteria are culturally biased. For example, testing which assumes knowledge of a predominantly white European interest might be discriminatory.

Remedies

Where there has been discrimination in the delivery of education, either by the education authority or an independent school, you have the right to complain, and/or to raise legal action in the courts. You should seek specialist legal advice from the Commission for Racial Equality or a solicitor.

Sex Discrimination

Sex discrimination can occur in two ways:

Directly – treating a person, on the grounds of their sex, less favourably than someone of the opposite sex in similar circumstances;

Indirectly – where a rule or condition which applies to everyone, actually affects one gender a lot more than the other, to their detriment, <u>and</u> this cannot be justified by other (lawful) reasons.

Direct discrimination can take many forms. In a school setting this might include sexist insults or comments, sexual harassment, or subtle differences in marking or treatment. The education authority and the school must take reasonable steps to protect your child from unlawful sex discrimination at school. If they do not, then the education authority may be held responsible for the discriminatory actions of another pupil or a visitor to the school.

Indirect discrimination can sometimes be justified by other (lawful) reasons. In schools, there should be an educational justification for differences of this type. Any potential justification must outweigh the disadvantage suffered by the people affected.

It is unlawful for schools to discriminate on the grounds of gender in any of the following:

• Decisions or policies on admission;

• Access to educational benefits, grants, bursaries, facilities, or other services;

• School meals, transport or uniform;

• Exclusions;

or by subjecting pupils to any other detriment or disadvantage.

In general, the education authority must not discriminate when carrying out any of its education functions and must make sure that facilities for education and any ancillary benefits are provided without sex discrimination.

Admissions

Schools which normally admit both boys and girls would be breaking the law if they refused to admit pupils on the grounds of their sex or made it more difficult for one sex. However, this does not apply to single sex schools or schools which are mostly single sex.

Accommodation

Schools with boarding accommodation for boys and girls are not allowed to refuse accommodation on the grounds of sex, but schools with accommodation for only one sex may do, even if they educate both sexes. Accommodation at mixed residences can be refused, however, if this would mean a pupil having to share sleeping, washing and other facilities with the opposite sex.

Exclusions

It is unlawful to sexually discriminate when excluding a pupil. Schools should make sure the same rules are applied to all pupils and that these do not unfairly disadvantage one gender.

Many more boys than girls are excluded in mixed gender schools. However this would only count as indirect sex discrimination if it was because the girls were being showed some sort of unfair preference.

There would be indirect discrimination if a school's decisions about exclusions affected proportionally more from one gender and this could not be justified on educational grounds.

Assessment

It is direct discrimination if your child is given lower marks because of his/her sex. This can come from overt prejudice, or unconscious assumptions about the relative abilities and characteristics of the sexes.

It might be indirect discrimination if assessment criteria are gender biased. For example testing which assumes knowledge of predominantly male interests might be discriminatory.

Dress and Uniform

Certain differences in uniform on the grounds of sex have been held to be lawful, as long as similar (though not identical) restrictions apply to the opposite sex. For example, it would not be unlawful sex discrimination to insist that girls do not wear trousers and that boys do not wear skirts.

Remedies

Where there has been sex discrimination in the delivery of education, either by the education authority or an independent school, you have the right to complain, and/or to raise legal action in the courts. You should seek specialist legal advice from the Equal Opportunities Commission or a solicitor.

Disability Discrimination

New disability discrimination duties (in force from September 2002) aim to protect disabled pupils by banning discrimination against them at school on the grounds of their disability. A disabled person is someone who has a physical or mental impairment which has a substantial and long term adverse effect on his/her ability to carry out normal day-to-day activities.

"Substantial" means more than minor or trivial; and "long term" means that it has lasted or is likely to last for at least 12 months or for the rest of the person's life.

"Physical or mental impairment" includes sensory impairments (such as hearing or sight impairments). Hidden impairments are also covered (for example, clinically well-recognised mental illnesses, learning disabilities and conditions such as epilepsy and Chrone's disease).

An impairment is said to affect your normal day-to-day activities if it affects one of the following:

Mobility;
Manual dexterity;
Physical co-ordination;
Continence;
Ability to lift, carry or otherwise move everyday objects;
Speech, hearing or eyesight;
Memory or ability to concentrate, learn or understand; or
Perception of the risk of physical danger.

What constitutes disability discrimination?

Disability discrimination may occur in two ways:

- by treating, without justification and because of their disability, disabled pupils less favourably than other pupils;

- by failing to make reasonable adjustments to avoid putting disabled pupils at a substantial disadvantage compared with other pupils.

However, there are some circumstances where the school would not have to make "reasonable adjustments", most importantly if it would mean having to provide auxiliary aids and services; or having to make alterations to the physical features of the school. The school would not have to do these things.

The provision of aids and adaptations is not dealt with in disability legislation, because it is assumed that these are covered in the Record of Needs.

The Scottish Executive is considering a planning duty to improve physical access to schools in Scotland.

It is unlawful for a school or education authority to discriminate against a disabled pupil in:

- Admissions policy or practice;

- Education or associated services provided or offered at the school; or

- Exclusion policy or practice.

Remedies

Where there has been disability discrimination in the delivery of education, either by the education authority or an independent school, you have the right to complain, and/or to raise legal action in the courts. You should seek specialist legal advice from the Disability Rights Commission or a solicitor.

Religious Discrimination

Although there is no specific law in Scotland against discrimination on the grounds of religious belief or affiliation, in education there is a limited amount of legal protection.

All publicly-funded schools must be open to pupils of all denominations – this almost certainly includes all religions, or those of no religion at all. Your child must not be put at any disadvantage if you have decided to withdraw him/her from religious education or observance.

The right of boarders at publicly funded schools to attend worship and otherwise practice their (or their parents') religion outside of school times is protected.

Human Rights

The Human Rights Act 1998 prohibits any discrimination which interferes with a pupil's right to access to education on any of the following grounds:

Sex;
Race;
Colour;
Language;
Religion;
Political or other opinion;
National origin;
Social origin;
Association with a national minority;
Property;
Birth; or
Other status (which includes disability)

See also

Consulting parents
Complaints
Exclusion from school
Legal action
Religious education and observance
Special educational needs

Where to find out more

"Higher Education and Equality: a guide" by the Equal Opportunities Commission and the Commission for Racial Equality.

"Equal Opportunities Guide for Parents" by the Equal Opportunities Commission (Scotland).

Legal references used in this section

Section 5 of the **Standards in Scotland's Schools etc. (Scotland) Act 2000**

Race Relations Act 1976

Race Relations Act 1976, as amended by the **Race Relations (Amendment) Act 2000**

Sex Discrimination Act 1975

Sections 9 and 10 of the **Education (Scotland) Act 1980**

Disability Discrimination Act 1995

Disability Discrimination Act 1995, as amended by the Special Educational Needs and Disability Act 2001

EXAMINATIONS AND ASSESSMENT

From the moment your child starts at school, they will be going through a process of assessment (albeit a fairly informal one). Your child's class teacher will make a regular note of his/her progress, and will tailor any individual learning programme to his/her needs. Each year, a formal record of your child's progress will be added to his/her school record. You will also be given the opportunity to keep up to date with your child's progress through parents' evenings and report cards. Outwith these times, your child's head or class teacher will be happy to discuss your child's progress with you. It is usually advisable to make an appointment though.

If the assessment process picks up on any concerns which may require additional support, the school will usually want to discuss these with you. Occasionally, children may be formally assessed with a view to establishing whether a Record of Needs should be opened for them. If this is the case with your child, you should be kept fully informed and involved.

Near the end of your child's second year at secondary school, you will be asked to choose which subjects he/she will take in the third and fourth years, with a view to sitting standard grades or acquiring other formal qualifications. Some schools will offer a very wide range of subjects at this stage, while others (usually smaller schools) may have a more limited range. If your child has a particular career in mind, you should find out from the careers service which subjects would be beneficial. The choice of subjects is a clear example of the type of decision about which a parent ought to consult their child. The school is not obliged to allow your child to take the subjects you have requested. If you feel strongly that your child should be allowed to take a particular subject, you should discuss this initially with the relevant class teacher, then with the head teacher. If you are still not satisfied, you may wish to take this up with the education authority.

Who is responsible for examinations?

Up until your child sits the formal Standard Grades, it is the education authority and the individual school who determine the timing and content of exams. They will also determine the timing and content of any 'prelim' exams your child sits.

It is the responsibility of the Scottish Qualifications Authority to devise and develop qualifications, to mark candidates and to award qualifications. It is responsible for the content and time-tabling of the actual Standard Grades and National Qualifications.

What examinations will my child sit?

At the end of fourth year, your child will normally sit Standard Grades. Standard Grades can be sat at three different levels:

Foundation (Grades 5-6),
General (Grades 3-4) and
Credit (Grades 1-2).

Usually, all pupils sit the general paper, and either the foundation or credit, according to their level of ability.

Once your child moves on to fifth and sixth years, a wide range of National Qualifications opens up, according to your child's ability. National Qualifications are offered at the following levels:

Access,
Intermediate 1,
Intermediate 2,
Higher, and
Advanced Higher.

Which level your child sits in a particular subject will depend to some extent on the level of award he/she obtained at Standard Grade, however your child's teachers will be able to give you and your child detailed advice.

It is now possible for particularly able pupils to sit Standard Grades at the end of S3 and Highers at the end of S4.

If your child is absent from an exam, for example due to illness (a medical certificate will usually be required) it is possible for them to be awarded a qualification on the basis of classwork and other supporting documentation.

Special arrangements (e.g. scribing) can be made for pupils who have a disability which could hinder them in an exam.

If your child does not achieve the grades he/she was widely expected to achieve, it is possible to appeal. This can only be done via the school however, not by the individual concerned. The school will provide supporting information such as prelim papers and classwork. If you think this may be appropriate in your child's case, you should contact the school as soon as possible to discuss this. If an appeal is successful, a new certificate will be issued.

See also

School records
Special educational needs

Legal references used in this section

Education (Scotland) Act 1996

EXCLUSION FROM SCHOOL

During 1998/99 there were 34,831 exclusions from schools in Scotland, most being temporary exclusions of male secondary school pupils.

Can the school just send my child home?

Schools cannot informally suspend or expel pupils. Any attempt to remove or ban your child from school is an exclusion and must be carried out according to certain procedures. This applies even where the removal is only for a brief period (e.g. sending him/her home early from school for misbehaving), or where the education authority has made provision for your child to be educated at another school.

The education authority almost always allows the head teacher and senior management team of each school to make decisions about temporary exclusions.

What about exclusion and human rights?

It is not, in principle, a breach of your child's human right to education to be excluded from school. However, if the exclusion has the effect of preventing your child from attending another school, then it may be a breach. Also your child must not be excluded on the grounds of your refusal to comply with school rules, if that refusal is based on a religious or philosophical conviction (such as a religious objection to a school parade).

Grounds for exclusion

The education authority may exclude your child from school (either for a short period or indefinitely) only where it thinks one of the following applies:

- You have not complied with the school's rules (including disciplinary rules) or have prevented your child from complying; or

- Your child's continuing attendance at school is likely to have a serious (detrimental) effect on the school's order and discipline or on the education of its pupils.

The grounds for exclusion, while covering a range of circumstances, are strictly limited in each case. The first cannot be used on the basis of your child's conduct alone; the second requires that his/her continuing attendance would have a "serious" effect on the life of the school. These circumstances should only arise relatively rarely.

Reasons for exclusion

The government's guidance says that it should only be in exceptional circumstances that any pupil would be excluded for any reason other than these:

fighting | physical abuse of pupils | physical abuse of staff
verbal abuse of pupils | verbal abuse of staff
aggressive/threatening behaviour | general/persistent
disobedience | insolent/offensive behaviour
drug-related incidents | racist incidents
lack of parental co-operation

Of course, the reason must also come within one of the two grounds for exclusion.

What about my child's education?

The fact that your child has been excluded from school does not necessarily excuse his/her absence, nor does it excuse you from your duty to have him/her educated.

If your child has been excluded from school, even temporarily, the education authority must arrange for him/her to receive education – either at another school or at home.

Procedures for exclusion

Where a decision to exclude has been taken, the school (or the education authority) must:

On the same day, in conversation or in writing:

> tell you that your child has been excluded; and
> arrange a meeting within seven days to discuss the exclusion with you.

Within eight days, in writing:

> tell you why your child was excluded;
> tell you under what conditions your child will be allowed to return to school (if any);
> tell you about your right to appeal and where any appeal should be sent; and
> give you any other relevant information.

If your child returns to school within seven days or you indicate within that time that you don't wish to appeal, the "eight days" letter is not strictly required.

These procedures are subject to strict time limits and the school must comply with them exactly. If the school does not stick to the procedures, then the exclusion may be overturned on appeal.

Conditions are commonly imposed for return to school. Usually, you and/or your child will have to it sign a document guaranteeing his/her future good behaviour. The courts have found this to be a lawful condition.

If your child is over school leaving age the information above must be given to him/her, instead of to you. If the school gives the information to you, it might be seen as a breach of your child's right to respect for his/her private life and correspondence. Children of about twelve years and over now have the right to appeal against their own exclusion, but the information on the right to appeal and how to do so would still be sent to you. It is good practice for copies of all the above information to be sent to your child also. Failure to do so might breach your child's right to an effective remedy, as he or she may not be able to access the right to appeal effectively without this information.

Alternatives to exclusion

Children who are excluded from school often fall behind with their work, which jeopardises their educational attainment further as they struggle to catch up. Additional funds have been made available to schools for in-school alternatives to exclusion, so that increasingly, exclusion should only be considered after other alternatives have failed, or for the most serious of disciplinary offences.

Does the school need to follow official guidance?

In 1998, the government published guidance about exclusion, which was meant to give some sort of consistency to exclusions throughout the country. Each education authority had to produce its own guidance, given to each of its schools to produce consistency within its area. You should be able to obtain a copy from your education authority.

These documents can be important because the education authority is, in effect, placing further restrictions on the way it carries out exclusions. It will usually include things like who can impose an exclusion and, importantly, a requirement that exclusion be used as a disciplinary measure of last resort. If a school does not stick to the guidance, then the exclusion may well be overturned on appeal.

I want to appeal against my child's exclusion

For the appeal procedures see the section on **Appeals**. You, or your child (if he/she is over school leaving age), have the right to appeal against an exclusion. In addition, children aged twelve or more, together with younger children of sufficient maturity and understanding, have the right to appeal.

Who do I make my appeal to?

Your appeal will be heard, in the first instance, by the education authority's appeal committee. After that you (or your child) have a further right of appeal to the sheriff court, whose decision is final.

What can they decide?

Both the appeal committee and the sheriff court have the same powers:

* to uphold the exclusion;
* to quash the exclusion; or
* to alter the conditions of return to school.

Neither can alter the length of an exclusion. An appeal to the sheriff court, while kept as informal as possible, is a complex legal procedure, and you should seek legal advice and/or representation from a solicitor familiar with education law. You or your child may be entitled to Legal Aid.

What will they take into account?

Nothing in the law says when an appeal should succeed or fail. The reported cases of appeals to the sheriff court are wildly different in their approaches, having taken decisions based on the following factors:

* whether or not the decision to exclude was justified at the time;
* whether or not the decision to exclude was reasonable;
* whether or not the decision involved an improper exercise of discretion;
* whether or not the appeal procedures had been properly followed; and
* whether or not any procedural flaws disadvantaged the pupil.

As you can see, there is no consistent approach, although it seems that an appeal to the sheriff court would not, in general, be a simple rehearing of the facts (as is the case with placing requests). It is more likely to involve at least some element of legal argument, so representation is highly recommended.

School Records

Education authorities include details of any exclusions on your child's school records. Details of previous exclusions will be used in making decisions about and appeals against new ones. Therefore, it is very important to appeal against any decision to exclude with which you disagree, no matter how short the period of exclusion is.

If the exclusion is overturned on appeal, then the note about it should be removed, or at very least amended to show that it was overturned on appeal.

Special Circumstances

Where a child is "looked after" by the local authority or is otherwise "in need" at the time of an incident which may lead to exclusion, the local authority's duties to that child may be relevant to the decision to exclude and to any appeal. The pupil's case social worker may also be informed of and become involved in the exclusion process.

Where it is proposed to exclude a pupil with recorded special educational needs, the case for exclusion must be balanced against the education authority's ongoing obligation to provide the education and support assessed as required in the Record of Needs. This may prove difficult if it involves the use of specialist equipment or staff only available at the school in question.

See also

Appeals
Choice of school
Leaving age
School records
Special educational needs

Where to find out more

"*First annual survey on exclusions from school in 1998/99*" by the Scottish Executive Education Department (2000).

"Guidance on Issues Concerning Exclusion from School" Circular 2/98 by the Scottish Office Education and Industry Department (1998). Available from the Scottish Executive.

"Social Inclusion – Opening the door to a better Scotland" by the Scottish Office (1999). Available from the Scottish Executive.

Legal references used in this section

Section 41 of the **Standards in Scotland's Schools etc. (Scotland) Act 2000**

Article 8, Schedule 1; Article 13, Schedule 1 of the **Human Rights Act 1998**

Sections 14(3); 28F(3),(4),(8)&(9); 28H(6)-(7) of the **Education (Scotland) Act 1980**

Reg 4 of the **Schools General (Scotland) Regulations 1975**

"Guidance on Issues Concerning Exclusion from School" – **SOEID Circular 2/98**

Wallace v. City of Dundee Council 2000 SLT (Sh. Ct.) 60

Mackie v. Grampian Regional Council 1999 FamLR 122

Crawford v. Strathclyde Regional Council 1999 FamLR 120

Inderhaug v. Grampian Regional Council 1999 FamLR 120

McDonald v. Grampian Regional Council 1999 FamLR 122

Valsamis v. Greece (1996) 24 EHRR 294

Wyatt v. Wilson 1994 SLT 1135

Yanasik v. Turkey (1993) 74 DR 14

X. v. United Kingdom; Appl. 13477/1987 Commission 4 October 1989

D. v. Kennedy 1988 SLT 55

Campbell and Cosans v. United Kingdom (1982) 4 EHRR 293

FEES AND CHARGES

School education provided by the education authority must be free of charge. You cannot be charged for tuition for courses taught in the school or for things like books, materials and equipment or other articles which your child needs to take full advantage of their school education.

Nursery education provided by the education authority must be free of charge for children of the ages set down by the law (approx. 3-5).

However, examples of when fees and charges can be made include:

The use of social, cultural or recreational facilities, such as community education premises, or sports or leisure equipment or centres.

Specialist lessons for music or other subjects if these are provided at a more advanced level than at other schools.

An education authority providing school education for a pupil who lives outwith its area. Any fees it charges will usually be met by the pupil's own education authority.

Education authority nursery or pre-school education which is over and above that which it has to provide by law.

Where a fee is charged for classes, then the education authority may also make a charge for books, materials or equipment needed for those classes.

Extra-curricular activities like school trips or additional tuition out of school times. However, these must always be optional, and suitable alternative arrangements must be available for those who do not take part in school trips (for example).

The education authority can award scholarships to any pupil in its fee-charging classes, to cover all or part of the fee. A scholarship may only be awarded on the grounds of the pupil's aptitude and ability.

Assisted Places

The assisted places scheme still exists for some pupils, but is being phased out. It provided financial assistance to parents unable to meet the full fees of a fee-paying school. No new assisted places may now be created and the last of the assisted pupils will have left by the end of the school year in 2005.

Independent Schools

Independent schools are, obviously, allowed to charge fees for education, limited only by what parents are prepared to pay.

See also

Books, equipment and materials

Pre-school education

Legal references used in this section

Section 33 of the **Standards in Scotland's Schools etc. (Scotland) Act 2000**

Sections 1(1C); 3(1); 3(3); 3(5)(b); 11(1); 23; 24; 75A of the **Education (Scotland) Act 1980**

FINANCE AND FUNDING OF EDUCATION

Local authority schools

Local authority schools receive the vast majority of their funding from the local authority itself. The local authority receives its funding from central government and from local taxation such as council tax. Each year, the council will make projections on how much it will need to spend during the next financial year in all of its departments. It then sets its council tax rates at a level which will make up the deficit between the amount of funding it will receive from central government and the amount it has projected it will need to provide services throughout the next year. Councils have a general duty to ensure that their resources are used economically, efficiently and effectively. Each year, local authorities must publish annual abstracts of accounts. You are entitled to a copy of these, although you are likely to be charged for the copy. If you object to anything in the accounts, on the basis that the money has been spent negligently or unlawfully, you can make written objections to the auditor within 14 days of the publication of the accounts.

It is very much in the discretion of the local authority how much of its revenue is spent on education, provided that it meets all of its statutory duties. The education committee will set the education budget for each financial year. This will take into account the money needed for salaries, books and equipment, and maintenance costs. You can get access to the reports and minutes of education committees and sub-committees, to find out what the expenditure projections and breakdowns are for the education budget.

Some local authorities have initiated "Public Private Partnerships" in a bid to improve the standards of education provision. This is a scheme which is supported by the Scottish Executive, whereby private companies either build new schools or carry out extensive improvements to existing schools and invest in modern technology. The local authority then leases the schools and equipment from them over a period of several decades. During this period, the private companies maintain the buildings and equipment, and are responsible for cleaning and other services. At the end of the lease period, the buildings will transfer to local authority ownership. Although the buildings are not owned and maintained by the local authority during the period of the lease, the authority has the same responsibilities towards the pupils attending these schools as it would if it did own the buildings.

Independent schools

Independent schools receive no funding from local or central government. They generate their income from the fees charged for pupils' attendance. Occasionally, a child may be placed in an independent school by an education authority. In this situation, the education authority will pay the school fees to the independent school directly.

Other sources of funding for schools

Both local authority and independent schools may receive other income or property from, for example, educational endowments (usually made by charities or foundations), bequests from private individuals, donations from individuals or businesses and from money raised by pupils and parents. Recently, some private companies have begun to sponsor certain facilities within schools (such as school canteens). You may be consulted if your school is considering taking on such a sponsorship, however there is no requirement for consultation. If you object to a proposed sponsorship arrangement, you could take this up with the head teacher or the education authority. In such a situation, it would be worthwhile finding out whether other parents also object. You may wish to raise this through your PTA/PA or school board if your school has one, or you may consider setting up a parents' pressure group if interest is high.

See also

Special educational needs

Where to find out more

"*A Simple Guide to Money Matters*" by the Scottish Parent Teacher Council.

FINANCIAL ASSISTANCE
(including grants and bursaries)

Education authorities can (but they don't have to) make payments to young people over school age who are staying on at school, if their families would experience financial hardship without it. The payments can cover the cost of any school fees, costs incurred in taking part in the full educational activities of the school, and the young person's maintenance expenses. An education authority can only make these payments to young people who stay within its area and who are British or EU nationals.

While education authorities are allowed to make such payments, they do not have to. In practice, however, most education authorities do have a scheme for making payments to young people whose parents are on low income or in receipt of benefits. You should contact your child's school or the education authority for further information.

Provisions relating to school clothing grants, assistance with travelling expenses and free school meals apply equally to pupils over school leaving age as to those under school leaving age.

See also

Clothing and school uniform
Meals and milk
Transport

Legal references used in this section

Section 49 of the **Education (Scotland) Act 1980**

The Education Authority Bursaries (Scotland) Regulations 1988

FLEXI-SCHOOLING

What is Flexi-schooling?

Flexi-schooling is where parents and a local school share the job of teaching a child in an agreed partnership set out in a contract drawn up between the two. Parents who would otherwise be quite content to home educate, may wish their child to be able to take advantage of certain educational resources only practically available through the school.

Flexi-schooling is practised by some local authorities in England & Wales, where the concept of authorised absences is provided for by law. There, as in Scotland, flexi-schooling is only possible with the active support and permission of the education authority.

Do I have a right to flexi-school?

Legally, if your child attends a local authority school, your obligation is to ensure he/she attends regularly. Any absence without reasonable excuse leaves you open to prosecution. There is no legal provision for a "third way".

Would an arrangement for flexi-schooling count as a reasonable excuse for non-attendance the rest of the time? Previous court cases would suggest not. However the definition of reasonable excuse may have to be revisited in light of the Human Rights Act. However, it is by no means certain that it would include this alternative form of educational provision.

On the other hand, parents' right to educate in accordance with their own wishes might be accommodated by a school if it treats certain pupil absences as if that pupil were present at school, and agrees to record them as authorised absences. This applies where the absence has been authorised and you comply with any conditions set by the education authority.

See also

Attendance and absence

Where to find out more

"*Flexischooling*" by Roland Meighan (contact Schoolhouse for details).

Legal references used in this section

Section 28(1) of the **Education (Scotland) Act 1980**

Reg 9; Sched 1 of the **Schools General (Scotland) Regulations 1984**

GUIDANCE

When guidance is needed

Children will from time to time need guidance from school or other staff about:

- their studies and which courses or subjects to choose;

- any personal problems they may be having at school; or

- choosing a career or deciding what to do after leaving school.

The education authority must have written information for parents about the guidance provided at each of its secondary schools. Specialist staff are appointed at secondary schools to provide guidance. In primary schools the head teacher or other staff may also be able to offer guidance.

Guidance teachers

All local authority secondary schools in Scotland have guidance teachers. Their job is:

- to help pupils decide about what subjects to choose for Standard Grades, Highers and other courses, and to monitor their progress and attainment (educational guidance);

- to help pupils with any personal problems, such as bullying or settling in (personal guidance); and

- to help pupils decide about careers and/or further or higher education (careers guidance).

Guidance teachers sometimes also teach programmes of personal and social education, which deal with health, relationships and careers. The law requires guidance teachers to act reasonably in advising pupils and responding to their questions or concerns, and to exercise ordinary skill and judgement. If they fail to meet this standard, the education authority may have to provide compensation for any injury or loss caused as a result.

Educational guidance

The education authority can offer guidance about the education it makes available to pupils. Most secondary schools will make arrangements to advise and consult pupils and parents about decisions relating to what subjects to study, what exams to take, and education after school leaving age.

Personal guidance

Children should be given personal guidance to help them cope with any problems they are having, including ones to do with settling in when starting school or moving school, study problems (e.g. poor concentration), or trouble with fellow pupils (e.g. bullying or victimisation).

Careers guidance

Careers advice and information must be made available to children before leaving school or further education to help them choose a suitable career. This should take into account your child's capabilities and the training needed for a particular career. Careers advice may continue to be given once your child has left school. A record must be kept of vocational advice given to your child.

Your child may be given the opportunity to go on a work experience course before leaving school.

Child guidance (psychological service)

The education authority must provide its own child guidance service, staffed by educational and child psychologists, trained to deal with any behavioural or learning difficulties. Child guidance staff have special responsibility for attending to any special educational needs your child might have, but they may also become involved if your child is having discipline problems in class. Your child may be referred by the school for clinical observation and you yourself can ask for an assessment which, if reasonable, cannot be refused.

See also

Careers education
Information for parents
Special educational needs

Legal references used in this section

Section 8 of the **Employment and Training Act 1973**, as amended by the **Trade Union Reform and Employment Rights Act 1993**

Sections 4; 61(1) and 61(6) of the **Education (Scotland) Act 1980**

HEALTH

Medical and dental examinations

The education authority has a number of rights and responsibilities in relation to your child's health. Firstly, it can ask you to present your child for medical or dental examination. It may do this, for example, if you have said your child is too ill to attend school. If you fail to comply with such a requirement, you could face prosecution.

Secondly, "in the interests of cleanliness", education authorities may authorise a medical officer to examine the bodies and/or clothing of all pupils, some pupils or an individual pupil. (Female pupils must be examined by a female medical officer). If the examination finds a pupil to be infested with vermin, or otherwise in a foul condition, then the education authority may issue a notice on the parent (or the pupil him/herself if over school leaving age) requiring treatment or cleansing to be carried out within 24 hours. If the problem is not put right within 24 hours, the education authority can then issue a notice requiring the pupil to be cleansed or treated, and this would give authority for the pupil to be treated. It is worth noting, however, that if your child has a sufficient level of understanding to consent to medical treatment and procedures, then any medical examination or treatment can only be carried out if he/she consents. This would seem to significantly water down the education authority's powers in this area, and may render them ineffective in relation to pupils over school leaving age.

If the medical officer has reason to believe that a pupil is infested with vermin or otherwise in a foul condition, but arrangements cannot be made for him/her to be examined or treated straight away, then the education authority may exclude the pupil from school until they can be examined or treated. If a pupil is excluded from school in these circumstances, then the period of exclusion will be seen as absence with a reasonable excuse, unless the pupil's infestation is as a result of some "wilful default" on the part of the parent or young person.

If a pupil is repeatedly found to be infested, this may lead to the parent's prosecution (or the pupil him/herself if over school leaving age). Repeated infestation may also be mentioned in grounds for referral to a children's hearing.

Immunisation

As part of the immunisation programme, arrangements are made for immunisation of children of school age to take place within schools. If your child is due to be immunised, you will be notified and should be given information about the proposed immunisation and given a consent form to complete and return. You are under no obligation to have your child immunised, and your child will not be immunised without consent (however, if your child is old enough to give consent him/herself, it would be possible for him/her to provide the necessary consent even if you had refused).

Health in the curriculum

As part of their general duties towards pupils, education authorities often introduce health issues into the school curriculum. For example, the dangers associated with smoking and drug and alcohol abuse, as well as sexual health matters may feature in your child's classes. The type of information your child receives will depend on what stage of schooling he/she is at.

See also

Attendance and absence
Children's hearings
Exclusion from school
Sex education

Legal references used in this section

Section 2(4) of the **Age of Legal Capacity (Scotland) Act 1991**, s2(4)

Section 57 & 58 of the **Education (Scotland) Act 1980**

Section 131A of the **Education (Scotland) Act 1980,** as inserted by the **Standards in Scotland's Schools etc (Scotland) Act 2000**

HOLIDAYS

School Holidays

Schools must normally stay open for 190 days (excluding Saturdays and Sundays) in the "school year". In Scotland, the school year normally runs from mid–August to late June or early July the following year. There are traditionally school holidays in the autumn, and at Christmas and Easter, plus various shorter one-day or long weekend holidays.

School opening, closing and holiday dates are fixed by the education authority, and it must inform parents of these dates. Different holiday arrangements may exist for different areas or schools within the same authority.

The education authority may alter the dates of the school session at its discretion. However, where it wants to make a drastic change to a long-standing holiday, it would probably have to consult with parents (and pupils) before doing so.

Independent schools are responsible for deciding their own opening and closing dates and holidays. They do not have to stay open for 190 school days, although the education authority will need to be satisfied that the education provided remains of an adequate and efficient standard.

For certain reasons the school may stay open for fewer than 190 days a year, for example, as a result of industrial action, fire damage, or some other reason beyond the education authority's control.

Family holidays

As a parent, you have a legal duty to see that your child continues to go to school regularly, except where there is a reasonable excuse for his/her absence (such as illness). There may be occasions, however, when you wish or need to take your child on holiday or away from school during term time.

You should write to the school asking permission to do this, and give the reasons for your request. If your child's attendance has been otherwise good, the request should normally be granted for a short holiday up to two weeks. Requests for absence for relevant religious holidays should also normally be granted. If you are refused permission, action may be taken against you for your child's non-attendance at school.

See also

Attendance

Where to find out more

"*Education Authority School Term Dates*" (current edition) by the Scottish Executive Education Department.

Legal references used in this section

Section 35 of the **Education (Scotland) Act 1980**

Schedule 1, Part II (o) of the **Education (School and Placing Information) (Scotland) Regulations 1982**

Reg 5(a) & (c); 9 and Sched 1 of the **Schools General (Scotland) Regulations 1975**

Para 6.3 of **SOED Circular 1/95**

HOME EDUCATION

Education is compulsory, but school is not. While you have to make sure your child is educated, you do not necessarily have to send him/her to school. Some parents choose to educate their children at home instead.

What is home education?

Home education is the term used for parents educating their children at home rather than by sending them to school. It covers a wide variety of styles of educating, from formal school-type lessons to a more flexible "child-centred" approach to learning.

In Scots law, a child's education is their parent's responsibility. Not for nothing are teachers sometimes described as acting "in loco parentis". Parents are under a duty to provide their children with education. Most parents fulfil this duty by sending their children to school. However, the law provides for two choices, each as valid as the other:

• your child attending a local authority school; or

• by other means (including independent schools and home schooling).

It is important to remember that the law says that, as a general rule, children should be educated according to their parents' wishes. The European Convention of Human Rights says that children are to be educated guaranteeing respect for their parents' religious or philosophical convictions. A commitment to home education could quite easily be a "philosophical conviction". Both of these rights are limited however by the requirement for the education provided to be "suitable" and "efficient". These terms are not defined in the law, and different people have different ideas about what they mean.

Do I need permission to home educate?

No, if your child has never attended a local authority school (i.e. has attended only independent schools or has been home educated): then you do not need any consent to home educate; but

Yes, if your child has attended a local authority school (even once): then you need the education authority's consent before you can withdraw your child from school. The education authority can take as long as it likes to reach a decision. During this time, you are legally obliged to make sure your child continues to attend school. This can be very difficult if your child is having problems at school.

Will the education authority still be involved?

Whether your child has been withdrawn from school or has never been, the education authority is likely to take an interest in your decision to home educate. Many parents resent this, seeing it as an unwelcome and unwarranted intrusion into their home. It is, however, unwise to be too dogmatic at this stage.

You do not have to allow the education authority to visit your home. However, it does need to be satisfied that the education you are providing is both efficient and suitable to your child's age, aptitude and ability. It is easier to demonstrate this at an early stage rather than in front of a committee of the education authority or the sheriff court.

What sort of education is required?

As mentioned above, the required standard of education ("suitable" and "efficient") has not been defined, either by Parliament or by the courts. In England, courts have ruled that a suitable education is one which "prepares children for life in a modern, civilised society" and an efficient education is one which "achieves what it set out to achieve". However, this is not binding in Scots law and it is just as likely that a Scots court would take a more restrictive approach. In fact, it is unlikely that a Scots court would ever be asked to decide what these terms mean, since the appeal cases on attendance orders suggest that they will look only at how the education authority exercised its decision-making powers, not at whether its decision is correct.

What are the education authority's powers?

The education authority must not refuse you consent to home educate without good reason. However, if the education authority is not satisfied that your child is receiving the required standard of education, it will ask you to appear before a committee to assess whether or not the education you provide meets the required standards (you can provide the information in writing instead).

If the education authority remains dissatisfied, then it must serve an attendance order on you, requiring you to send your child to the school named within it. You have the right to appeal against this to the sheriff court, but an appeal is only likely to be successful if the education authority has improperly exercised its decision-making powers. This is a complex area and you should seek expert legal advice on the subject.

The European Court of Human Rights has decided that it is not a breach of your rights to respect for your philosophical convictions to require you to co-operate with an assessment of your child's educational attainment.

The Scottish Ministers are to issue guidance for education authorities about the circumstances in which parents may choose to educate their children at home.

Is home education a "reasonable excuse" for not attending school?

If you withdraw your child from school without consent, or an attendance order has been issued, the education authority will argue that your child is not attending school "without reasonable excuse". A recent court case means that the concept of what is a "reasonable excuse" can be redefined under the

Human Rights Act. This means that it may be possible to argue that home education could be counted as a reasonable excuse, in certain circumstances.

If your child is not attending school without reasonable excuse then the education authority can take criminal legal proceedings against you or refer your child's case to the Reporter to the Children's Panel.

See also

Appeals
Attendance and absence
Children's hearings

Where to find out more

Schoolhouse Home Education Association

Legal references used in this section

Section 14 of the **Standards in Scotland's Schools etc (Scotland) Act 2000**

Schedule 1, Part 2 of the **Human Rights Act 1998**

Section 53 of the **Children (Scotland) Act 1995**

Sections 28(1); 30 and 35(1) of the **Education (Scotland) Act 1980**

North Lanarkshire Council v Rae, Airdrie Sheriff Court, 12 January 2001 (see 2001 SCOLAG 49 for commentary)

Parlane v Perth and Kinross Joint County Council 1954 SLT (Sh Ct) 95

Family H v. United Kingdom (1984) 37 DR 105

Harrison & Harrison v. Stevenson (Worcester, 1981)

(H)

HOMEWORK

The law has next to nothing to say on the subject of homework. Schools do not have to set homework, nor can they be forced to do so by legal action. Local authority schools must publish written information for parents about their policy on homework.

Almost all schools will set homework on a regular basis, but will vary in the amounts, level and type of homework given. HM Inspectorate of Education expects that homework will be set. It is seen as a way of improving the quality, range and appropriateness of teaching. Homework should be used effectively, be well planned and linked to classwork.

It is probably lawful for a school to make a reasonable level of homework a compulsory part of its school education. If so, then a pupil could be subject to discipline for failing to complete homework

See also

Discipline and punishment
Exclusion from school
Information for parents

Legal references used in this section

Schedule I, Part II (e) of the **Education (Schools and Placing Information) (Scotland) Regulations 1982**

HUMAN RIGHTS

The Convention for the Protection of Human Rights and Fundamental Freedoms was signed by the United Kingdom in 1950. Until 1999, it had no direct application in the United Kingdom, and the only way British citizens could access the rights it gave them was to take action in the Court of Human Rights in Strasbourg. This was a very lengthy process.

The Human Rights Act 1998 came into force on 2 October 2000, and has far reaching implications. The main changes it led to are:

• *Every public authority must act in accordance with human rights.* A "public authority" is any body that carries out functions of a public nature, and includes courts and tribunals.

• *When courts are interpreting legislation, they must do so in a way which is compatible with human rights.* If they find that a piece of legislation is incompatible with human rights, they will issue a "declaration of incompatibility". This, however, does not invalidate a piece of Westminster legislation, it only draws parliament's attention to the defect.

The Scottish Parliament is only allowed to make laws which comply with human rights.

The relevant human rights are:

The Convention for the Protection of Human Rights and Fundamental Freedoms:

Article 2:	Right to life
Article 3:	Prohibition of torture
Article 4:	Prohibition of slavery and forced labour
Article 5:	Right to liberty and security

Article 6:	Right to a fair trial
Article 7:	No punishment without law
Article 8:	Right to respect for family and private life
Article 9:	Freedom of thought, conscience and religion
Article 10:	Freedom of expression
Article 11:	Freedom of assembly and association
Article 12:	Right to marry
Article 14:	Prohibition of discrimination (in the application of Convention rights)
Article 16:	Restrictions on political activity of aliens
Article 17:	Prohibition of abuse of rights
Article 18:	Limitation on use of restrictions on rights

1st Protocol:

1:	Protection of property
2:	Right to education (so far as is compatible with the provision of efficient instruction and training, and the avoidance of unreasonable public expenditure.)
3:	Right to free elections

6th Protocol:

| 1: | Abolition of death penalty |
| 2: | Death penalty in time of war |

Human rights and education

The application of human rights in education is yet to be tested in Scotland, and it is not clear how courts will interpret it. It is likely that articles 8, 9, 10 and 11 will lead to most challenges. The right to education in Protocol 1 is a very general right, and the provisions of the Education (Scotland) Act 1980 and the Standards in Scotland's Schools etc (Scotland) Act 2000 probably go beyond what is required of this provision. Examples of cases which have been taken to the European Court of Human Rights in the past include school uniforms, corporal punishment, religious education and the education of travellers.

Decisions made by education authorities, further and higher education institutions, grant-making bodies, education appeal committees, children's hearings and courts will all have to conform with human rights. At this stage, it is unclear whether independent schools will be seen as carrying out a function of a public nature, and so it is not clear whether they ought to act in accordance with human rights.

If you successfully challenge a decision which did not conform with human rights, you may be awarded damages.

If you feel that you or your child's human rights have been violated by a public authority, you should seek legal advice as soon as possible. Any action claiming a violation of human rights must begin within a year of the incident complained about.

It is still possible to take a case to the European Court of Human Rights, however given the length of time such a case would take to be decided, this is not a particularly effective remedy.

Where to find out more

The Scottish Human Rights Centre

INDEPENDENT SCHOOLS

Can I send my child to an independent school?

Any parent is entitled to seek a place at an independent (or private) school for their child. You do not have to send your child to a local authority school if you can satisfy the authority that you have made adequate alternative arrangements of your own for your child's education. You simply write to the independent school of your choice asking for an application form and information about the school and its fees. Your child will probably have to attend an interview and may have to sit a school entrance examination or test before being offered a place.

Organisation and courses taught

Independent schools vary greatly in their character and size and in the range of pupils admitted. Some are different in their educational approach from others or have special interests like creative arts. Some provide schooling from age 5 or pre-school right through to school leaving age and beyond. Some take in boys or girls only, and some are mainly for boarders. A number cater exclusively for children with special educational needs or disabilities. Others cater specially for children with special abilities and aptitudes, for example in dance, drama and music. Most independent schools will offer a range of courses and subjects very similar to local authority schools, and enter pupils for the same examinations. Classes in independent schools are often smaller than those in local authority schools.

Registration of independent schools

Any person, group of people or organisation (including parents and parents' organisations) can set up a school. Any school (other than a local authority one) which offers full-time education for five or more children of school age must be registered as an independent school.

Registration will be refused if the proprietor, the premises or any teacher of the school has previously been disqualified. It will also be refused if the Scottish Ministers notify the Registrar that they think:

• the proprietor is not a proper person to be a proprietor of a school;

• any teacher to be employed there is not a proper person to be a teacher in a school; or

• the premises (or any part of them) are unsuitable for use as a school.

The school may appeal.

Registration is on a provisional basis only until an inspection has been carried out and the proprietor given notice that final registration has been granted.

The register of independent schools is a public record and contains the name, address and proprietor of each independent school in Scotland. It is a criminal offence to run an independent school which is neither registered nor provisionally registered.

Inspections

Independent schools, like local authority ones, are open to inspection at any time. Inspectors have to be satisfied that:

• efficient and adequate education is being provided for pupils there;

• the school is owned and staffed by suitable people;

• the school's premises are suitable and accommodation adequate; and

• the welfare of the pupils attending the school are adequately safeguarded and promoted.

Failure to meet these requirements could result in removal of the school from the register.

Complaints

You may at any time make a complaint to the Scottish Ministers about an independent school. You may want to do this, for example, if you think it is being badly managed, or your child's welfare is not being looked after well enough. You should seek advice before making a complaint. If your complaint is accepted, the Scottish Ministers must give the school at least six months to put matters right or to face removal from the register. The school can make an appeal about such a decision to an Independent Schools Tribunal. If the complaint is about an individual teacher then that teacher must be named and notified of the complaint.

The Tribunal can:

• annul the complaint;

• order that a school be struck from the register;

• give the school a certain date to put matters right to the satisfaction of the Scottish Ministers;

• disqualify the person(s) you are complaining about from running or teaching in any school; and

• disqualify the premises from being used as a school.

Your legal rights

If you have sent your child to a fee-paying school, you will be in a contractual relationship with the school. You have agreed to pay fees in exchange for educational services. Just as the school could sue you for breach of contract if you did not pay the fees, so you may be able to sue the school for breach of contract where the services provided are deficient in some way. You should seek legal advice before you consider such action.

See also

Inspections and inspectors' reports

Where to find out more

The Independent Schools Information Service provides information about independent schools across the UK. They provide a series of free leaflets, such as planning an independent education, questions to ask when visiting a school, school fees, scholarships and grants, etc.

Legal references used in this section

Sections 30; 66; 98; 99 and 100 of the **Education (Scotland) Act 1980**

Registration of an Independent School (Scotland) Regulations 1957

INFORMATION FOR PARENTS

Getting to know about the school

As a parent you are entitled to receive written information about your child's school, if it is run by a local authority, whenever you ask for it or are offered a place there. The type of information you are entitled to is laid down by law, and falls into 3 categories:

• basic information;

• school information; and

• supplementary information.

Basic information

Basic information is intended mainly for parents thinking of choosing an alternative school for their child (other than the local school). This must include information about how the education authority goes about:

• offering school places to pupils, including priorities for admissions where placing request demand exceeds available spaces;

• arranging for the admission of pupils who have not reached school starting age; and

• providing school meals, transport and boarding accommodation.

For each school the basic information must cover its name, address, telephone number, approximate roll, stage(s) of education provided, denomination (if any) and the gender of pupils admitted.

The information must also include addresses and telephone numbers of education and divisional education offices and contact points for parents who want more information or who think that their child has special educational needs . Basic information does not have to include information about nursery schools or classes, although you are entitled to this information if you ask for it.

School information

School information is intended for parents of children already attending or about to attend a particular school or who want to choose a school in another area. This information must cover:

- the name, address and telephone number of the school, its present roll, stages of education provided, denomination (if any) and the gender of pupils admitted;

- the name of the head teacher and the number of teaching staff. Nursery schools or classes must also give the number of nursery nurses, and special schools must also give the number of specially qualified staff;

- arrangements for parents whose children are offered or are seeking a place at the school to visit it;

- the school's educational aims;

- details about the curriculum, including the school's policy on homework and the provision of religious education and observance and parents' rights in that regard. Secondary schools must also mention the courses they provide, personal and careers guidance, and arrangements for parents to be consulted about school subject options and choices;

- the school's arrangements for assessing pupils' progress and making pupils' progress reports available to parents;

- out-of-school hours activities;

- school sports and outdoor activities and facilities available;

- the school's policy on uniform and clothes and the approximate cost of each item of required uniform;

- the school's policy on discipline, school rules, and the enforcement of attendance;

- arrangements for providing meals, including entitlement to free school meals and where to apply for them, also facilities for eating packed lunches;

- arrangements for medical care;

- organisation of the school day, including arrival and dismissal times, school term dates, and holidays for the forthcoming session; and

- (for primary schools) the name, address and telephone number of the school to which pupils will normally transfer when they go on to secondary education;

Secondary schools (other than special schools) must also:

- say how pupils are grouped into classes for different subjects (i.e. mixed ability, ability sets, split classes etc.);

- set out their policy on entering pupils for public examinations; and

- give the number of pupils passing exams conducted by the Scottish Qualifications Authority, including details of the year group and grades;

Special schools must provide information about what particular children are catered for, and what specialist services are available.

Supplementary information

Supplementary information is intended for parents wanting additional information for a variety of reasons but which is not given out as a matter of course. You are entitled to receive on request supplementary information about:

- *school admission arrangements*: school catchment areas, names of "feeder" primary schools and "receiving" secondary schools, and where pupils normally go from schools which do not cover all stages of primary or secondary education;

- *choice of school*: parents' rights to request an alternative school, the circumstances in which such requests can be refused; parents' right to appeal; any guidelines issued by the education authority for admitting pupils to schools or nursery classes where placing request demand exceeds available places;

- *school rolls*: how the education authority decides the maximum number of pupils for each school or stage;

- *rights of parents and young people to appeal* against certain decisions about special educational needs;

- *the education authority's policies and practices* on: what is taught, assessment and exams; pupils with special abilities; school meals; school clothing and uniform; bursaries, grants and other financial help; discipline and other school rules; pupils with special needs; and school boards;

- *names of nursery schools* and nursery classes, with addresses, telephone numbers and approximate rolls;

- *names of special schools* not run by the education authority but to which they normally send pupils, including for each school the name address and telephone number, current roll, stages of education covered, the special needs catered for, and specialist services provided; and

- *names of schools in which Gaelic is taught.*

Where will I find this information?

Basic information

The education authority must let you see the basic information at any of its schools, main or divisional education offices and, if possible, public libraries in its area. This information only has to be about schools in that local area.

You are entitled to be sent the information free of charge if you live in the education authority area, if you are to move to the area, or are considering sending your child to school there.

School information

The education authority must give you a copy of the information about a particular school as soon as your child is offered a place there or whenever you ask for the information. This will often be in the form of a school handbook or prospectus, and must be given free of charge. You are entitled to receive information about any number of schools run by your education authority or by other education authorities.

Basic and School information

The basic and school information must be brought up to date each year and state which year it is for. It must also be published in Gaelic (in Gaelic speaking areas) or other languages if necessary.

Supplementary information

The education authority must give you any supplementary information you ask for if you live in or are to move to its area or are considering placing your child in a school there. The information can be given verbally or in writing, although you can insist that it is confirmed in writing. Information about your legal appeal rights must be confirmed in writing. A map of a school's catchment area must be available at each school and at the head or divisional education office.

Supplementary information may be available in places such as public libraries, but also at each individual school for its own information.

Annual statement of education improvement objectives

Each year the education authority must publish its objectives for improving education, within the current national priorities in education and performance indicators (as defined by the Scottish Ministers). It must consult with parents' groups (among others) when preparing the statement. It must include details of how the education authority will try to involve parents in promoting the education of their children. An annual report on its success (or otherwise) in meeting these objectives must also be prepared.

School Development Plan

Each year the education authority must prepare, for each of its schools, a school development plan. The development plan sets objectives for each school based on the annual statement of education improvement objectives. The development plan must be prepared after consultation with (among others) the school board, and any parents' groups for that school. Again an annual report must be prepared to show what has been done to put the plan into practice within the school.

Parents of pupils at the school are entitled to free access to the plan and the report on request (and to a free copy of their summaries).

Review of School Performance

The education authority must, from time to time, assess the quality of each school's education against its own measures and standards for judging performance. Where a school fails to meet the standards, the education authority must take action to put right the problems.

When deciding the measures and standards of performance, the education authority must consult with parents' groups and others. The measures and standards must be published.

Parents' Charter - Your rights to information

Under the Parents' Charter, you have further rights to information about your child's school and other schools. For example, you can compare exam results for every secondary school in Scotland.

You also have rights to regular information about your child's educational progress, and about the school's policies and curriculum. School reports should provide details of your child's attainment and progress. They should also describe clearly the targets your child is working towards.

New reporting procedures for primary and early secondary schools mean that reports should now:

tell you about your child's attainment in each subject in relation to national standards;

give details of the national tests your child has taken in English and maths;

describe your child's general development at school and their next steps;

allow you to comment on what the report says; and

allow you to discuss the report with your child's teacher.

In secondary school, your child has a right to information, advice and guidance about education and employment choices. The school guidance and careers service provide this information.

Information about your child's school

All schools must produce a handbook by 15 December each year. This tells you about the school, its organisation, what it teaches, its achievements, and its policies on discipline, school uniform, homework and so on. This should include all the basic and school information relevant to that school.

Other information about schools

Education authorities must send to all parents of pupils in Primary 7 tables which compare the secondary schools in their area. These tables must give information on examination results, destinations of school leavers, school costs for each pupil and attendance and absence rates.

See also

Appeals
Careers education
Choice of school (including placing requests)
Guidance
Special educational needs

Where to find out more

See the Parent Zone web site (address at the end of the book).

Legal references used in this section

The **Education (Schools and Placing Information) (Scotland) Regulations 1982**

Sections 4, 5; 6 and 7 of the **Standards in Scotland's Schools etc. (Scotland) Act 2000**

INSPECTIONS AND INSPECTORS' REPORTS

Her Majesty's Inspectorate of Education (generally known as HMIE) is part of the Scottish Executive Education Department and has the power and the task of inspecting all schools and educational establishments in Scotland. This includes nurseries, primary, secondary and residential schools, and further education establishments. You will normally be told in advance that your child's school is to be inspected, although some types of inspection are carried out without notice.

There are 4 types of inspection carried out:

• Nursery school, class or pre-school inspection

• Standards and Quality inspection (primary and secondary)

• Care and welfare inspection

• Care and welfare of residential pupils inspection

The areas covered by the inspection include:

• The views of parents, pupils and staff

• Staffing levels, accommodation and other resources

• The curriculum and pupils' academic performance (including performance in external examinations)

• How the school provides for the welfare of its pupils

Can I tell the inspectors what I think?

Parents have the opportunity to take part in an inspection by completing a questionnaire about the school. There is also provision for a random selection of pupils to take part in the inspection.

After the inspection

Following an inspection, the HMIE will produce a report. A copy of this report will be sent to each parent with a child at the school. Within 4 months of the publication of the report, the school and the education authority will issue an action plan detailing how they will deal with any points raised in it. Usually within 2 years of the publication of the HMIE report, the Inspector will carry out a follow up inspection to see how well the points in the action plan have been implemented.

Education authorities, as well as schools can now be inspected to review the way in which they are exercising their functions as to the provision of school education. This can be a general inspection, or can look into specific aspects of the education authority's functions. The education authority must give all reasonable assistance to whoever is carrying out the inspection.

In addition to the inspection of individual schools, HMIE analyses the results of its inspections on a national level, in order to inform the Scottish Ministers and Scottish Executive of the current and future educational issues to help them improve the quality of education throughout Scotland. Sometimes the Scottish Ministers or the Scottish Executive will ask HMIE to carry out investigations into specific topics related to educational matters. The HMIE also uses the expertise it has developed to provide professional advice on education to education providers and other bodies.

LEAVING AGE

You are required to make sure that, as long as your child is of school age (whether they attend school or not), you provide efficient education for him/her that is suitable to his/her age, ability and aptitude.

There are two school-leaving dates:

> Summer leaving date – this is 30 May. If your child turns 16 between 1 March – 1 October, he/she can leave school at the summer leaving date.

> Winter leaving date – this is the first day of the Christmas holidays (or if your child is not being educated within a school, 21 December). If your child turns 16 between 1 October – 1 March, he/she will have to wait until the winter leaving date before they can leave school.

Although children are allowed to leave school once they reach school leaving age, they are also allowed to stay on at school. Education authorities have the power to make payments to pupils for whom staying on at school may cause financial hardship.

Once a child reaches school leaving age, they are legally termed a "young person" (rather than a pupil) and many of the legal rights of parents transfer to them (such as the right to receive notifications about exclusion from school). In the case of children with special educational needs which render them unable to exercise their rights as a "young person", the parents retain their rights even although the child has reached school leaving age.

LEGAL ACTION

A last resort

While it is possible to take legal action, for example to make the education authority carry out its statutory duties, it is important to see such action very much as a last resort, only after attempts at an amicable solution have failed. Sometimes taking legal action can damage relationships between parents and schools, and you should consider carefully balancing what can be achieved by taking legal action against any negative effects on your child's education. It is also worthwhile bearing in mind that court actions can take some time (perhaps even years) to be completed.

Who can take legal action?

Where duties are owed to you (e.g. provision of information about schools), a legal action can be raised in your name. Where the legal duty is owed to your child (e.g. right to school education) the action should be raised in his/her name. Any child who is able to understand what consulting a solicitor and raising a court action means can do so in his/her own right. There is a presumption that children aged 12 and over have this level of understanding. If your child is too young to consult his/her own solicitor, then you can do so and raise a court action on his/her behalf.

If your child attends a non-local authority school (e.g. an independent school) then many of the rights you have will depend on the individual contract you have made with the school, rather than on the law. In this case, you, rather than your child (as your child is not a 'party' to the contract) would have the legal rights to raise an action.

Do I need a solicitor to take legal action?

No, you do not *have* to employ a solicitor to take legal action, but it can be very difficult (in many cases virtually impossible) for people to successfully negotiate the legal maze.

Different kinds of legal action

There are a number of different kinds of legal action which can be taken in relation to education matters. The most common of these are:

Judicial review

This type of action can only be raised in the Court of Session in Edinburgh. It is a way of challenging a decision made by an education authority or other public body, where no other means of appeal is available. For example, if an education authority fails to fulfil a statutory duty (e.g. the right of a child to be provided with school education) or if it has an element of discretion, but exercises this unreasonably.

Appeals

The process for appeals is set out in the law. This includes exclusion, placing request, special educational needs and attendance order appeals.

Compensation claims

If someone has been injured (either physically or psychologically) because of someone else's fault, negligence or failure to fulfil a statutory duty, then the injured person may be entitled to financial compensation. Examples of this could include a child injured because of a lack of supervision within the school. It would also be possible to claim compensation for lack of educational attainment or employment prospects if an education authority has failed, for example, to provide appropriate educational provision for a child or has failed to effectively tackle bullying.

However, this type of case can be very difficult to prove, and you will almost certainly need specialist advice and representation to take this type of action.

Interdict

This is a way of preventing the education authority doing something which it is not allowed to do.

Human Rights issues

If you believe that an education authority or other public body has infringed your or your child's Convention rights, then you can raise this as part of one of the types of court action described above, or you can raise a court action relying solely on the human rights argument.

Action which can be taken against you

There are many instances where action can be taken against parents (and young people). For example, prosecution and/or referral to a children's hearing for a failure to make sure your child keeps attending school regularly; failure to submit your child to medical examination; or failure to provide suitable education for your child. If legal action is taken against you then you should seek legal advice as soon as possible.

Financing legal action

Funding is available for legal advice and representation from the Scottish Legal Aid Board (SLAB). Eligibility will depend on your income and any capital you have. Your solicitor will be able to advise you on whether you are financially eligible. The majority of children will be eligible on the financial criteria. SLAB offers two basic schemes:

"Advice and Assistance" covers any work the solicitor has to do before taking a case to court. It also covers advice about appeal committee hearings, although it will not pay for a solicitor to represent you at an appeal committee hearing.

"Civil Legal Aid" covers the work which a solicitor will carry out when conducting a court case, such as a compensation claim, judicial review or interdict.

See also

Advice and assistance
Appeals
Complaints
Human rights

MEALS AND MILK

The education authority has powers to provide milk, meals and other refreshments to pupils at its schools (e.g. a school canteen). Except for free school meals (as below) it must charge for these and must charge each pupil the same price for the same things. The education authority must provide facilities for pupils to have food and drink brought by them to the school (e.g. a dining hall for packed lunches).

Education authorities also have the power to provide milk, meals and refreshments at other schools, though this is rarely, if ever, done.

Free School Meals

Education authorities must provide, free of charge, sufficient milk, meals and other refreshments in the middle of the day for pupils at their schools who are, or whose parents are, in receipt of Income Support, Income-based Jobseekers' Allowance, or support under the Immigration and Asylum Act 1999.

In 1997, 22% of all nursery and primary pupils were entitled to free school meals. For secondary pupils the figure was 16%. The rate of take-up, however, was lower than those figures. There is thought to be a certain amount of stigma attached to free school meals which is at least partly responsible for the low take-up. Some local authorities have introduced procedures which provide anonymity for those who get free school meals (including electronic "smart" cards). Where anonymity is not ensured, you or your child may be able to take legal action on the basis of human rights.

It is up to you (or your child) to bring your entitlement to free meals to the attention of the education authority.

The education authority must provide written information on its general policy on school meals, and the arrangements made at each school.

There have been proposals to extend the availability of free school meals, and it remains to be seen what will become of these.

See also

Human rights

Legal references used in this section

Immigration and Asylum Act 1999

Sections 53 and 55 of the **Education (Scotland) Act 1980**, as amended

Education (School and Placing Information) (Scotland) Regulations 1982

MEDICAL ATTENTION

As a general rule, only those people with parental responsibilities for a child can consent (or withhold consent) to medical treatment or attention for their child. This includes mothers, fathers who are or have been married to the child's mother, and unmarried fathers and others who have acquired parental rights and responsibilities through a court order.

In emergency situations, someone over 16 who is only temporarily caring for a child but has no parental rights or responsibilities in relation to him/her may consent to medical treatment if this would be reasonable to safeguard the child's health, development and welfare (and provided he/she has no reason to believe the parent would refuse consent). This provision does **not** however extend to someone who has temporary care or control of a child in a school. This means that teachers will not be allowed to consent to medical treatment, even in an emergency situation, in your absence. When you enrol your child at school, you will be asked for emergency contact numbers and these will be kept on your child's school record. In a case of real emergency – a life or death situation – a doctor will be able to carry out lifesaving treatment on your child even if there is no-one present who is able to consent to the treatment.

If your child requires assistance in taking medication at school, or other regular medical attention at school, you will have to complete a consent form, authorising staff members to carry this out. This consent form will be kept on your child's file. If your child has particular health needs or difficulties which could affect his/her ability to take part in certain activities or classes, you should inform the school and they will take these into account.

If your child is going on a school trip you will probably be asked to sign a consent form in case your child requires medical treatment. The staff who accompany children on school trips are responsible for their safety and supervision, and if your child requires extra attention or help with medication, you should advise the school well in advance.

See also

Health

Legal references used in this section

Sections 1; 5(2) and 11 of the **Children (Scotland) Act 1995**

MIGRANT AND OTHER MOBILE CHILDREN

The education authority's duty towards children in its area

An education authority has a duty to provide education to all the children in its area, regardless of whether the children are nationals of the UK, EC or some other state. Similarly, the parents of such children are under an obligation to ensure their children are educated (whether at school or otherwise).

Children of mobile workers

If you work away from home a lot, the education authority can either provide boarding accommodation for your child while you are away or arrange for the education authority in the area where you are staying to provide education on your "home education authority's" behalf. It is under no obligation to do so, and in deciding whether to exercise its discretion in this matter, will take into account what other provisions you could make for your child's care and what would be in your child's educational interests.

Travelling children

If travellers feel that the education authority's policy towards school education for their children is discriminatory, they may be able to challenge the policy on the basis of the Race Relations Act 1976, as some travellers groups have now been recognised as coming within the Act's remit. Similarly, education authority policies may be challenged as contravening articles 8 (right to respect for family and private life) and/or 9 (freedom of thought, conscience and religion) of the human rights Convention.

Children from other EC states

Children from other EC states and their parents can expect the same education rights as their British counterparts. In addition, they are entitled to free English tuition, and help with adapting to their new country. There is also a duty to promote teaching in the child's mother tongue, and instruction in the child's culture of origin.

Children moving out of the area

If you are moving permanently to another education authority area in Scotland, your new education authority will owe you and your child the same duties in relation to education as your last one (although the way education authorities interpret and implement their duties may differ). The law relating to education in England, Wales and Northern Ireland is slightly different to Scots law. However, if you are moving to any of these countries, you can expect your child to have the same rights as other children living in your new area.

If you are moving abroad, but within the EC, you and your child will have the same rights as the nationals of the member state you are moving to, with additional rights for your child to receive tuition in one of the official languages of that particular country.

If you are moving abroad, and outwith the EC, your and your child's rights will depend very much on the domestic law of the country you are moving to, and you should check the position with the country's Embassy or High Commission.

Where to find out more

"I didn't come here for fun: listening to the views of children and young people who are refugees or asylum-seekers in Scotland" by the Scottish Refugee Council and Save the Children (2000).

"Traveller Pupils and Scottish Schools" Spotlights no. 76 by the Scottish Council for Research in Education (2000).

"Refugee Pupils in Scottish Schools" Spotlights no. 74 by the Scottish Council for Research in Education (1999).

PARENT-TEACHER AND PARENTS' ASSOCIATIONS

There is an increased and increasing emphasis on parental involvement in schools and in education generally. One common way in which parents can become involved in what's going on at their child's school is through a Parent–Teacher (PTA) or a Parents' Association (PA). Generally there is little difference between the two, although as the name suggests, a PTA will tend to have teachers as members as well as parents. There is no legal requirement for PTAs or PAs to be set up within schools, although some education authorities do encourage this. In addition, school boards must encourage the formation of parents' associations and parent–teacher associations.

With the introduction of statutory requirements for parents to be consulted about local authorities' annual statements of educational improvement objectives and school development plans, this may lead to an increase in the number of PTAs and PAs which are set up.

PTAs and PAs can become involved in a wide range of activities. Many are devoted solely to fundraising activities, while others take an active interest in educational and other matters affecting the school.

It is advisable to have a formal document or "constitution" setting out the aims of the association, how often meetings are held, how office bearers are appointed, etc. This is particularly the case if the association will be handling any money. PTAs and PAs are publicly liable for their actions, with members of their committees carrying the liability personally. The Scottish Parent Teacher Council gives advice to PTAs and PAs on, among other things, how to set up an association and about insurance.

If a school doesn't have a PTA or PA, it is open to any parent to go about setting one up. The initial steps would be firstly to establish whether there is a willingness among fellow parents to become involved, and secondly to approach the school board (if there is one) and the head teacher to see if he/she would be agreeable to setting one up. The more parents who are keen to set up an association, the more likely the head teacher is to agree.

Most schools allow their PTAs or PAs to meet on school premises free of charge. However, they are not obliged to do so, and may charge for accommodation or withdraw co-operation altogether.

See also

School boards
Consulting parents

Where to find out more

Scottish Parent Teacher Council

Legal references used in this section

Sections 5 and 6 of the **Standards in Scotland's Schools etc. (Scotland) Act 2000**

Section 12(1) of the **School Boards (Scotland) Act 1988**

POST-16 EDUCATION AND LIFELONG LEARNING

Once pupils reach school leaving age, they are free to choose whether to stay on at school, go on to further education, take up a training place or find employment. Pupils with a Record of Needs will have a future needs assessment carried out before they reach school leaving age to make recommendations about whether they would benefit from continued school attendance.

Staying on at school

Pupils can generally stay on at local authority schools beyond their school leaving age, usually up to the age of 18, but sometimes longer. If staying on at school may cause the pupil or his/her family financial hardship, the education authority can pay the pupil a bursary to allow him/her to take part in the full activities of the school and to cover their maintenance expenses.

Further and higher education

Education authorities can establish further education colleges within their area. Further education colleges offer a wide range of courses, from recreational ones to courses which lead to formal qualifications. While you will need formal qualifications to get on some of the courses on offer, many require no formal qualifications. There is an increasing emphasis on "lifelong learning", encouraging adults to continue learning long after they are of school leaving age. In addition to full time attendance, many courses are offered on a part-time, evening or flexible basis. There is also an increasing number of distance learning and internet based courses available. For many full time courses, financial assistance by way of bursaries or loans may be available, and students with children or other dependents may be eligible for additional assistance. If you are considering taking up a college course, you should contact the college in the first instance to find out what type of financial assistance will be available.

Right to time off for education and training

Anyone aged 16-17 who is in employment and has not achieved a minimum number of standard grades, SVQ's etc has the right to a reasonable amount of paid time off work to study or train for a relevant qualification.

See also

Special educational needs

Where to find out more

"*Further and Higher Education Charter for Scotland*" by the Scottish Office. Available from the Scottish Executive.

"*What Support is Available for Young Scottish Students in Higher Education*" (current edition). Scottish Executive.

"*Further and Higher Education in Scotland*" Subject Map by the Scottish Parliament (August 1999).

"*What Support is Available for Mature Scottish Students in Higher Education*" (current edition). Scottish Executive.

"*Student Support in Scotland: a guide for undergraduates*" by the Student Awards Agency for Scotland (2001).

PRE-SCHOOL EDUCATION

The Scottish Executive recognises that for many children aged 3-5, pre-school education can provide the ideal grounding to prepare them for the transition to full time education. It has therefore set targets that there should be free nursery provision for all 3 and 4 year olds whose parents wish to take this up. A new curriculum framework has been produced for 3-5 year olds, which all nursery providers who receive funding through this Scottish Executive initiative are expected to follow.

Does the education authority have to provide nursery schools?

At present, there is no legal obligation on education authorities to provide nursery schools or classes, although all of them do. However, the Scottish Ministers will shortly have powers to impose a legal obligation on education authorities to provide nursery education. It is anticipated that this will come into force at some point in 2002.

What if there are not enough places?

If demand for places outstrips supply, priority will be given to children who have a greater need for nursery placement. For example, children who have special educational needs identified at an early stage may be given priority for a nursery place. There is also an obligation on local authorities to provide day-care for children who are "in need", if this is appropriate. Children in need includes children who are subject to a supervision requirement issued by a children's hearing, those who are unlikely to achieve a reasonable standard of health or development without input from the education authority, and children affected by disability.

Do I have to send my child to nursery?

No, you do not have to send your child to nursery.

However, if there were concerns about the level of care your child was receiving at home, the social work department and/or other professionals may advise you that your child's needs would be best met by taking up a nursery place or day care place. In exceptional cases, if you ignored this advice, this may form part of the grounds for referral to a children's hearing on the basis of a lack of parental care or of neglect. It would be open to the children's hearing, if they felt it was in your child's best interests, to insert a condition to their supervision requirement that he/she attends nursery school regularly. If such a condition was in place, then you would be required to send your child to nursery, and the case would be brought back to the children's hearing quickly for reconsideration if you did not comply.

Transport

If your child is attending a local authority nursery school, the authority may provide transport, but there is no legal obligation on them to do so. In the case of children attending day care provision, transport is often provided.

Where to find out more

"*Working with Children: a guide to qualifications and careers in early education, childcare and playwork.*" by the Scottish Executive.

"*Learning in the Pre-School Year: a parent's guide*" by the Scottish Office (1998). Available from the Scottish Executive.

PROPERTY LOSS AND DAMAGE

Who is responsible for taking care of pupils' personal belongings?

Your child is responsible for taking reasonable care of personal belongings he/she brings into school. Depending on your child's age, you should exercise care in what he/she brings to school.

Where the school has taken items of property into its safekeeping, then it must take reasonable care of those items and may be liable in compensation if they are damaged or stolen. These circumstances could include:

• Coats and bags left in cloakrooms;

• Valuables entrusted with teachers during physical education;

• Bicycles left in a designated area within the school.

The school also has duties not to cause damage or loss to your child's property by its own negligence (or that of its employees). For example, if a science demonstration was improperly supervised and your child's jumper was burned or stained, you may have a claim against the school.

What are children allowed to take into school?

The school can say in its school rules what sort of personal property may or may not be brought into school or lessons. Pupils may risk being disciplined for bringing prohibited items into school. Obvious examples would be cigarettes, alcohol, illegal drugs, or weapons.

Schools may also forbid or confiscate items which are interfering with schoolwork, such as handheld games consoles, mobile phones or Pokémon cards. (This must be balanced against article 1 of the 1st Protocol to the European Convention on Human Rights, which protects the right to the peaceful enjoyment of one's possessions). Articles taken away from pupils must be returned when the child leaves the school premises. Not to do so could count as theft. The school may hand over to the police any illegal items.

Can I claim for loss or damage?

You may be able to make a claim on your own insurance for loss or damage to your child's property, depending on the terms of your insurance. Where the school can be shown to be at fault, you should be able to claim against the education authority (or proprietor in the case of an independent school). Remember that just because something is damaged at school doesn't necessarily mean that the school is to blame. You may have to seek legal advice on bringing court action.

See also

Discipline and punishment
Legal action

RELIGIOUS EDUCATION AND OBSERVANCE

All schools (with the possible exception of independent schools) must be open to pupils of any religion or denomination. It has long been the custom in Scottish schools for religious observance to be practised and instruction in religion to be given to pupils. The law recognises this custom and the freedom for parents to withdraw their pupils from these elements of schooling without other disadvantage. The law states that education authorities are free to continue this practice.

Neither "observance" nor "instruction" are defined in legislation, but instruction would be found in lessons on religious education, whereas observance would include religious assemblies and other acts of worship.

While religious observance and instruction are not compulsory, where they are in place, they cannot be stopped without a local referendum in favour of that. Guidance has been issued as to the type and content of any religious observance and instruction. The law only says "religious", but this refers in most cases, to Christian religion. For example, a change from Christian religious observance to another form of religious observance would almost certainly also require a local referendum.

You have the right to withdraw your child from religious observance and from any education in religious subjects. This might include certain lessons from classes in subjects other than RE. Your child must not be placed at a disadvantage because of their (or your) denomination or religion, nor because of being withdrawn from classes or observance.

Your power to withdraw your child from religious elements of schooling is in line with the provisions of the Human Rights Act regarding the parent's right to have their children educated in accordance with their own religious or philosophical convictions. However, this might cause a conflict with a child's own right to freedom of thought, conscience and religion. The Scottish legislation at present indicates that the parent's will should take precedence, but it might be possible to challenge this assumption in the courts.

Children boarding at schools under the management of an education authority must be given reasonable opportunities to practice or be instructed in the religion of their parents' choice outside of school hours. Again this may cause a conflict where the child's religious beliefs do not coincide with those of their parents.

See also

Children's rights
Human rights
Legal action

Legal references used in this section

Schedule 1, Part II, Article 2 and Schedule I, Part I, Article 9 of the **Human Rights Act 1998**

Sections 8, 9 and 10 of the **Education (Scotland) Act 1980,** as amended

RESIDENTIAL (FORMER "LIST D") SCHOOLS

A residential school is a school with boarding accommodation where children who are experiencing difficulties are required to stay. Most children who attend residential schools do so under the authority of a children's hearing. A small number of children will be there because of an order from the Sheriff or High courts, or by voluntary arrangement with their parents. Generally speaking, children who are placed in residential schools will have a level of social work involvement.

Most admissions to residential school will be on a planned basis, with children and their parents having had the opportunity to visit the school, meet staff and residents and talk over any questions they may have.

Teaching

The schools usually offer much smaller classes than mainstream schools, and tend to have a more limited range of subjects, although there is usually provision for children to sit standard grade exams or obtain vocational qualifications. They are staffed by both teachers and care or residential staff, who are able to offer the young people the additional support they need.

Contact with your child

If your child is placed in a residential school, the local authority has an obligation to maintain and encourage contact between you and your child. Arrangements can also be made for your child to have contact with siblings and other family members. Contact arrangements should normally be discussed before your child is placed in the residential school. If a children's hearing authorises your child's placement in a residential school, then before coming to their decision, they must consider what contact arrangements are necessary. Most children in residential schools will have home leave, although the withdrawal of home leave is often used as a sanction for misbehaviour.

Corporal punishment

Corporal punishment is not allowed in residential schools, although staff in residential schools are trained in restraint techniques which are used if residents are behaving in a way which poses a risk to themselves or others.

See also

Children in care
Children's hearings

Legal references used in this section

Section 17 of the **Children (Scotland) Act 1995**

SAFETY AND SUPERVISION

Schools must take reasonable care of their pupils and look after their safety. Depending on the circumstances, certain precautions must be taken. These will have to be greater than would be expected for adults in the same situation.

Safety and supervision in schools

The education authority must provide supervision by at least one adult (eighteen plus) in a playground during any break time. This applies in every local authority school which is either:

• a primary school with fifty or more pupils; or

• a special school of any size.

The education authority must also take reasonable care for the safety of pupils under its charge. This includes the supervision of pupils, where that is needed to provide the reasonable care required. The duty to take reasonable care for the safety of pupils "under its charge" would include:

• on the school bus;

• on school trips;

• at school sporting events.

It is unlikely to include pupils who leave school at lunchtimes (especially if that is with your permission). It would not include pupils who arrive at school very early or leave long after the school day has ended unless pupils are attending school clubs/activities outwith normal school hours.

Standard of supervision

The law had previously required schools to act *in loco parentis* and to take care of pupils to the same standard as you would as a parent. More recently, this has been seen as an unhelpful and unrealistic standard of care to expect, where, for example, a head teacher is in charge of a school of several hundred pupils, or a class teacher is dealing with the supervision of twenty or thirty adolescents.

The most recent cases suggest that the school (and its teachers) have a duty to take reasonable care for the safety and health of children in their charge, and to exercise care and forethought, having regard to their age, inexperience, carelessness and high spirits, and the nature and degree of danger, not to subject them to unavoidable risk of harm.

Teachers are expected, while supervising pupils, to come up to the standard of a teacher of ordinary skill acting with ordinary care.

A greater degree of supervision may well be required where there is a greater risk of injury (e.g. certain science lessons involving dangerous materials, or physical sports).

The law has recognised a need to take into account the nature of some pupils, including "a tendency to meddling and mischief". However, schools are not expected to foresee "every act of stupidity" that might take place as a result. This approach recognises that pupils may often contribute to their own injuries, and the school cannot be entirely to blame in those circumstances.

Safety of buildings

The education authority (or independent school) must make sure that the school buildings and equipment meet current safety requirements. This means, for example, that the school should have well-sign-posted exit routes for evacuation of the building in the event of a fire or other emergency. The school should also carry out fire drills regularly.

Occupiers' Liability

The Occupiers' Liability (Scotland) Act 1960 creates a duty on the education authority to anyone who is lawfully on the premises (this includes pupils). The reasonableness of the care is assessed from the point of view of the pupil, so (especially in primary or special schools) extra care is required to prevent injury from features of the school premises.

Bad weather

Following cold weather, there is often a risk of injury from slipping. The education authority has a duty to pupils in its schools, to take reasonable steps to minimise the risk of injury (e.g. by spreading salt on the ice). The authority's duty of care applies regardless of the weather conditions.

Legal action

Where the school has failed to meet the required standards of supervision (as explained above) it would then be legally responsible for any reasonably foreseeable consequences. This means that you (or your child) could take legal action against the school if your child was injured as a result of the school's lack of adequate supervision, even where he/she may also be partly at fault. You should seek legal advice as soon as possible. You or your child may be entitled to Legal Aid.

Where to find out more

"*Safe School Trips*" by the Scottish School Board Association.

Legal references used in this section

Fire Precautions Act 1971

Reg 3 (a) & (b) of the **Schools (Safety and Supervision of Pupils) (Scotland) Regulations 1990**

Ahmed v. City of Glasgow Council; 2000 GWD 26-1004

Scott v. Lothian Regional Council 1999 RepLR 15

Murphy v. Bradford MDC [1992] PIQR 68

Beaumont v. Surrey C.C. (unreported, 1968)

Nicolson v. Westmorland C.C.; The Times, Oct. 25, 1962.

Perry v. King Alfred School Society (1961) The Guardian, Oct. 28

Cooper v. Manchester Corp.; The Times, Feb. 13, 1959

SCHOOL BOARDS

School boards are made up of parents, school staff and "co-opted" members, and are involved in the running of the school. They have a special duty to promote good relationships between the school and parents, and they have a number of other basic functions laid down in law. They can be given additional, "delegated" functions. School boards must exercise all their functions with a view to raising standards of education in the school and must support the efforts of those managing the school to improve the quality of education provided. Each school (other than a nursery school) should have its own school board, financed by the education authority. The size of each school board varies according to the size of the school.

Home-school communication

School boards have certain duties to promote parental involvement in school education.

> The board must encourage home-school contact, school links with the local community, and the formation of parents' associations and parent-teacher associations (PAs or PTAs).

> The board must find out as often as it thinks necessary what parents' views are on matters it is dealing with. It may, for example, want to consult parents about school book spending, curricular matters, school discipline, policy on homework and so on.

> The board must report back to parents of pupils at least once a year on its activities. The board can do this through meetings with parents, through written reports or both.

The head teacher must provide the board with information about the school's arrangements for parents and teachers to meet or consult one another. The head teacher must also consider and reply to any points of view from the board about these arrangements.

Parents' meetings

If enough parents ask, the board must arrange meetings of parents to discuss its activities or to propose resolutions. The request for a meeting must come from at least 30 parents of pupils or from a quarter of those entitled to vote at the last election of parent members of the board, whichever is less. Parents must say in writing why they want the meeting and what matters they wish to raise or which resolution they want to propose.

Only parents of pupils at the school may vote on resolutions. The board must consider any resolution passed at the meeting, although it need not act upon it.

Information and reports

The education authority must provide the board with any information it reasonably requests from time to time about its school, or about the authority's provision of education.

The head teacher must provide the board, as soon as it has been set up, with statements of the school's policies on:

• the curriculum,

• the assessment of pupils,

• discipline,

• school rules, and

• the wearing of uniform.

The head teacher must also advise the board of any changes in these policies, although he/she need not do so until those changes have actually taken place.

The head teacher must also issue an annual report to the board, including a report on the level of attainment of pupils in the school (but not on the attainments of individual pupils).

Advice to boards

The head teacher has the right, and, if requested by the board, the duty to give it advice on any matter it is concerned with. The education authority must also do so if requested by the board. The board must consider any advice given, although it need not necessarily act upon that advice.

The head teacher is also entitled, but not required, to attend meetings of the board. The director of education, nominated officials of the education authority, and councillors for electoral wards within the school's catchment area can also speak at and attend meetings. They are not members of the board and the board is not bound to accept any advice they may give. Councillors may not become members of school boards in their council area, even if they would otherwise qualify as parent, staff or co-opted members.

Books and materials

The education authority must provide the head teacher each year with money for schoolbooks and other teaching materials. It must also provide money for "other purposes" as it thinks fit. The school board is responsible for approving the head teacher's proposals for spending this money. If the board does not approve the proposals, the head teacher will have to submit new or modified proposals.

The school board and the head teacher must have regard to any guidance given by the education authority. They must also take account of any of the authority's policies on the school curriculum and make sure that the authority's legal obligations are met, for example, the duty to secure "adequate and efficient" school education.

Financial information

The education authority must by a certain date each year provide the school board with a statement on the school's running costs (e.g. on salaries, repairs and maintenance) and capital expenditure (e.g. on improvement work and new buildings) for the previous and the current financial year. Regulations set out what financial information should be presented. The authority must consider and reply to any comments the board may make about this information. The authority must also provide the board with any other financial information it reasonably requests.

Financial powers

The school board can raise funds (except by borrowing), spend the money raised, and receive gifts, so long as this is for the school's benefit and the head teacher is consulted. The board must keep proper accounts of its expenditure.

The education authority must provide the board with funds to cover administrative expenses, training and other expenditure.

Use of school premises

The school board is responsible for controlling the use of school premises outwith school hours. It has a duty to encourage the "community" use of school premises. This could include use of the school by voluntary organisations, for example. The board must, however, follow any directions given by the education authority, which continues to fix charges for the use of the school, except when this power has already been delegated to the board.

Occasional holidays

School boards, after consulting the education authority, can fix occasional holidays during school term time. There are legal limits to the number of days schools may be closed for holidays.

Delegated functions

School boards can be given additional responsibilities, known as "delegated functions". These might include taking charge of the repair and maintenance of school buildings, enforcement of school attendance, administration of staff salaries or other school expenditure, determination of school policy on discipline and so on. These functions can only be delegated at the initiative of the education authority, and only if the board agrees.

Functions can be delegated for a limited or for an indefinite amount of time. The authority can lay down conditions under which the delegated functions must be carried out.

Certain functions may not be delegated:

The board cannot take formal responsibility for employing or dismissing school staff (teaching or non-teaching).

The board cannot formally select head teachers, or depute and assistant head teachers (although the board is involved in selecting these members of staff, as described below).

The board cannot control the curriculum or the assessment of pupils (but the way in which results of assessments are reported to parents can be delegated).

The board cannot close down the school, move the school to another site, or merge the school with another one.

The board cannot end or set up special classes or a stage of education at the school, such as nursery or sixth year classes.

The board cannot decide on policies for admitting pupils to the school.

Under certain circumstances, the education authority can suspend, end ('revoke') or modify a delegation order. Certain procedures must be observed by the authority before this can be done. If necessary, the matter can be referred to the Scottish Ministers.

Appointment of senior staff

The school board must be represented on the committee set up by the education authority to appoint senior school staff: head teachers, depute head teachers and assistant head teachers. The committee interviews candidates for the post and recommends who should be appointed. The education authority must normally accept the committee's recommendations, which could include a recommendation to re-advertise. Equal numbers of school board and education authority nominees must sit on the committee.

For the head teacher appointments the committee must be chaired by one of the education authority's nominees, and for the other appointments, the committee must be chaired by the head teacher of the school. Staff members of the school board or co-opted members who are pupils at the school may not sit on the appointments committee.

For head teacher appointments, the authority will draw up a short-list of candidates, which must first be submitted to the school board before it is considered by the appointments committee. The board must meet without its staff and any co-opted pupil members to consider applications. The education authority must take the board's views into account.

See also

Consulting parents
Holidays
Parent-teacher and parents' associations

Where to find out more

The Scottish School Board Association

Legal references used in this section

The **School Boards (Scotland) Act 1988**, as amended by the **Education (Scotland) Act 1996** and the **Standards in Scotland's Schools etc. (Scotland) Act 2000**

School Boards (Scotland) Regulations 1989

SCHOOL BUILDINGS

Standards for schools

School buildings, like any other public buildings, must be built according to certain standards and requirements, including health and safety. The sort of buildings provided are determined by:

Building standards and regulations laid down by the government. Planning permission must also be given by the local authority before a school can be built or altered. Building standards cover things like the resistance of building materials to fire, access and escape routes, structural stability of the building, accommodation, drainage and supply of services (water, gas, electricity). Any extensions or improvements must also meet the latest building standards.

Health and safety requirements. Education authorities have to maintain and equip their schools in such a way that any occupants or visitors to the school premises are in healthy surroundings. They must obey any directions from the government for this purpose. People occupying or in charge of school premises must take reasonable care to make sure that anyone entering or using the building will not suffer damage or injury which may arise because of the condition of the building. This might, for example, involve keeping pupils out of classrooms while repairs are being done. The Scottish Ministers can make rules about the use of dangerous materials or apparatus in schools.

Special regulations for school premises. Apart from the normal building and health and safety regulations, education authorities must in addition provide school premises and sites that meet other requirements.

These requirements cover:

School sites and playing fields. The minimum size of school sites and playing fields is worked out according to a legally prescribed sliding scale based on pupil numbers. For example, a secondary school with 751–1,000 pupils must cover a site of at least 2.4 hectares. Nursery schools and classes must have a garden or playing space nearby; minimum standards are also laid down for the amount of playroom accommodation there. However, the Scottish Ministers can relax or modify these requirements if they consider them unreasonable or impracticable for particular schools.

School meals accommodation. Adequate and suitable accommodation must be provided for serving school meals and for washing up, even if the meals are cooked outside the school premises.

Washrooms. A sliding scale, based on pupil numbers, lays down the number of toilets, etc. In nursery schools and classes, for example, there must be one toilet for every 10 pupils. Except in nursery schools and classes, each toilet should be lockable and partitioned to ensure privacy. Disposal facilities for sanitary towels must be provided in schools with girls beyond primary 4 classes.

Medical rooms. Every school must have a room or other suitable place for carrying out medical inspections, except when the Scottish Ministers allow inspections to take place elsewhere. The medical room must have a toilet and a wash basin with hot and cold water. A rest room with adjacent toilet and hot and cold water supply must be provided in every secondary school.

Storage and drying accommodation. Cloakrooms and lockers must be provided for storing pupils' belongings and for hanging and drying their outdoor clothing. Every school must have sufficient storage space for books and materials, furniture, and fuel.

Outdoor areas. Playgrounds or other outdoor areas must be provided right beside the school building and be properly laid out and surfaced.

Lighting. Both natural and artificial lighting must be provided. There are technical specifications which give the minimum amount of light which must reach desk tops and other working surfaces. Light fittings must be positioned in order to prevent excessive contrast or glare in normal working conditions. There must also be protection against glare from the sky and sun.

Heating, ventilation and acoustics. Detailed specifications are laid down about room temperatures and ventilation in school buildings. For example, classrooms must have a minimum of 17°C, based on readings taken three feet from the floor, and be well enough ventilated, having regard to the use they are designed for. Classrooms and other parts of the school must be suitably insulated against noise and other disturbances.

Water supply. Proper drinking water must be supplied and there must be warm water for washing in. Warm showers must have a temperature of at least 30°C but no more than 44°C.

See also

Books, equipment and materials
Meals and milk
Safety and supervision

Legal references used in this section

Chapter 6 of the **Education (Amendment) (Scotland) Act 1984**

Chapter 44, sections 1 and 19 of the **Education (Scotland) Act 1980**

Chapter 37, sections 2 – 4 of the **Health and Safety at Work Act 1974**

Chapter 3 of the **Occupiers' Liability (Scotland) Act 1960**

School Premises (General Requirements and Standards) (Scotland) Regulations 1967/1199 as amended by **Statutory Instruments 1973/322 and 1979/1186**

SCHOOL CLOSURES AND CHANGES

Can education authorities close down or make other changes to schools?

An education authority has considerable power to close down or make certain other changes to schools. Before making its decision, however, the authority must give parents and others a chance to give their views on the proposals. In certain cases, the education authority may need consent from the Scottish Ministers as well.

Do parents and others have any say in the matter?

The education authority must seek the views of various groups of people before deciding whether to close a school down or to make certain other "prescribed" changes. Those it must consult are:

> **Group 1:** the parents of every pupil attending the school in question;
> **Group 2:** the parents of every child expected to attend that school in the next two years;
> **Group 3:** the school board (if there is one);
> **Group 4:** the authorised representative of the church or denomination (if it is a denominational school).

It is also possible for others to put their views to the education authority, although the authority will not necessarily have to take their views into account.

When there is a proposal to close or alter a school, parents of pupils of **any** school affected by the closure or change, must be consulted (not just the one to be closed or changed).

The education authority might also be expected to consult more widely as its decision might be unreasonable if it did not. For example, it may consult the wider community in which the school is located, teachers and other staff employed at the school.

What proposed changes require consultation?

The following groups of people (as listed above) must be consulted whenever the education authority proposes:

closing down a school or ceasing a stage of education within a school (i.e. one complete year group or all nursery classes);	Groups 1-4
providing a new school;	Groups 1-4
moving a school to a new location;	Groups 1-4
altering a school catchment area or making a new one;	Groups 1-4
changing which secondary school primary pupils transfer to;	Groups 1-4
providing an additional stage of education at a school;	Groups 1-4
providing or altering a special class for pupils with special needs at a mainstream school;	Groups 3 & 4 + parents of pupils moving school as a result
altering the arrangements for admission to a school based on ability, aptitude etc.;	Groups 1,3 & 4
changing a single-sex school into a co-ed school or vice versa or swapping the gender admitted;	Groups 1,3 & 4
changing the age or timing of transfer of pupils from primary to secondary education;	Groups 3-4
increasing or decreasing the number of school starting dates for pupils starting primary school;	Groups 3-4

making or changing guidelines for admission to certain schools where placing request demand exceeds available places;	Groups 3-4
fixing or changing the maximum number of pupils to be educated at a school or stage of education;	Groups 3-4
withdrawing transport or assistance with travel costs from children attending denominational schools;	Group 4
converting a denominational school into a non-denominational school.	Group 4

If the education authority makes major changes in its provision of education or related duties (meals, transport, boarding accommodation, uniform, discipline policies, school hours, etc.), it may face legal challenge if it does not provide adequate notice and consult those likely to be affected, even if it does not have a specific obligation to consult on these.

How should parents be consulted?

The education authority will send parents notification of the proposals, and allow 28 days for representations or comments to be received in response. The notice must also inform you of where you can get full details of the proposals. It may also give notice of any meeting to be held for parents to discuss them. Any such meeting must be at least 14 days after the notice and at a time and place convenient to parents outside normal working hours. The notification can be posted or sent home with the child, but it must reach both or all "parents" (including guardians and anyone else with parental responsibility for the pupil). For parents of children not yet at school, notification may have to be by advertisement in a local newspaper.

Proposed changes to the age or timing of transfer from primary to secondary education; the starting date for primary school admissions; and guidelines for priority of admission by placing request to a particular school must always be announced in the local press, giving at least 28 days to respond.

A school board or denominational body must receive the full details of the proposal and, again, have 28 days to respond.

The education authority must take into account all representations it receives about a particular proposal, having regard to the general principle that, so far as it is compatible with suitable instruction and training and avoids unreasonable public expenditure, children are to be educated in accordance with the wishes of their parents. Failure to properly and fully take these matters into account may lead to the decision being overturned by judicial review.

Is the education authority's decision final?

In certain cases the education authority must first get permission from the Scottish Ministers before carrying out certain proposals. These are:

• Any proposal which means a primary school pupil attending a school at least 5 miles (by the nearest available route) away from the previous school;

• Any proposal which means a secondary school pupil attending a school at least 10 miles (by the nearest available route) away from the previous school;

• Any proposal which means that a child at a denominational school has to attend a non-denominational school; and

• (where the denomination has objected) any proposal leading to a significant deterioration in denominational schooling compared to non-denominational schools run by the education authority.

See also

Consulting parents
Legal action

Legal references used in this section

Section 22A of the **Education (Scotland) Act 1980**

The **Education (Publication and Consultation Etc.) (Scotland) Regulations 1981**

Martyn Imrie for Judicial Review of a decision of Comhairlie Nan Eilean Siar (16 July 1999, Outer House, Court of Session P25/14G/99)

Harvey v. Strathclyde Regional Council 1989 SLT 612

SCHOOL DEVELOPMENT PLANS

Each year the education authority must prepare, for each school it manages, a school development plan. The development plan sets objectives for each school based on the annual statement of education improvement objectives.

The school development plan should say clearly how the school aims to improve its standards. It should show clearly what the school will do to improve pupils' attainments and the quality of their experiences at school. It should set down the targets it aims to reach, and review how well previous targets were met (or not). It should also say what the school's priorities for improvement are.

The development plan must be prepared only after consultation. An annual report must be prepared to show what has been done to put the plan into practice within the school.

Parents of pupils at the school are entitled to free access to the plan and the annual report on request (and to a free copy of their summaries).

A school development plan is not a legally binding document, it is more like a statement of the school's aims and how it will try to get there. Having said that, school inspectors look at the development plan as part of their inspections and if a school were consistently failing to have regard to its own development plan, that would be a legitimate reason for complaint.

See also

Complaints
Consulting parents
Consulting pupils

Legal references used in this section

Section 6 of the **Standards in Scotland's Schools etc. (Scotland) Act 2000**

SCHOOL RECORDS

Will records be kept about my child?

A progress record must be kept for every child who attends a local authority school. This record can only be used for supervising your child's educational development and for giving advice and assistance to, or about, your child. This means that it should not be shown to people like employers, social workers, or the police. The record is confidential and may only be disclosed to certain specified people.

What information is in the records?

The progress record must have the following information:

• Your name and address and the name and address of your child (if different);

• An alternative emergency contact;

• Any previous schools your child has attended;

• The dates and results of any objective, diagnostic, psychological or aptitude tests (including compulsory primary test results);

• Anything which might hinder your child's educational abilities or attainment;

• Your child's health record;

• Information about your child's emotional and social development (including, where appropriate, relationships with other pupils or teachers);

• Your child's yearly educational progress report; and

* For secondary school pupils, details of any posts of responsibility held in school or other related organisations.

What happens to the records when my child leaves school?

If your child changes schools, the progress record must be transferred to your child's new school, if they want it. The education authority has to keep a progress report for at least five years after your child has left school.

Who can see the records?

The following people can ask in writing to see the progress record together with any other educational records kept by the education authority:

* *You*, where your child is under eighteen, or is incapable of understanding the information requested; or

* *Your child*, where he/she is able to understand what exercising their right means (in Scotland, a child of 12 years is assumed to be mature enough to have such understanding).

When can I see the records?

The education authority must provide, free of charge, access to the information within forty days of receiving your written request. This does not include information which came from a health professional, where the education authority must first obtain the opinion of the health board or health professional as to whether the disclosure of the information would be likely to cause serious harm to the physical or mental health of your child or anyone else; or would lead to the disclosure of the identity of another individual. Neither does it include information which came from a Reporter to a Children's Hearing, where the education authority must first obtain the opinion of the Reporter as to whether the disclosure of the information would be likely to cause serious harm to the physical or mental health of your child or anyone else; or would lead to the disclosure of the identity of another individual; or would be likely to interfere with crime prevention, detection or prosecution.

If the information is about exam marks, and it is requested before the results of the exams are announced, the education authority has 5 months from receiving your request, or 40 days from the announcement of the results (whichever is earlier) to provide you with the information.

Where the disclosure of the information would lead to the identification of another person, that person must give his/her consent first, but the education authority must provide as much of the information as it can without needing consent within the forty days anyway.

What information can be withheld?

The education authority doesn't need to supply the information requested where the information:

- Is kept by a member of staff for his/her own use only;
- Is a reference given on behalf of your child for a job, college place etc.;
- Is part of a Record of Needs;
- Is covered by rules of legal privilege (e.g. solicitor's client confidentiality);
- Has been supplied to the education authority on a legally confidential basis;
- If disclosed would be likely to cause serious harm to the physical or mental health of your child or anyone else; or
- If disclosed, would be likely to interfere with crime prevention, detection or prosecution.

What if there is inaccurate information?

Where you or your child think that something in his/her records is wrong, you or he/she can write to the education authority to ask for the record to be corrected. You must say what you think is wrong, why you think that it is wrong and how it should be corrected. The education authority must either correct it as you suggest, or add a note of your objection to the record.

Where the education authority has refused to supply you with information, or to correct the record, you (or your child) have the right to request a review in writing within 28 days. The review will be heard by a sub-committee of the education committee. You (or your child) can put your case in person or in writing.

Record of Needs

The information contained within a Record of Needs is strictly controlled due to the confidential nature of the documents. The principal copy of the Record of Needs remains with the education authority, while a copy is sent to you (or your child if he/she is old enough), and another copy to the school, where it forms part of your child's progress record.

If the Record is amended or modified then you must be notified. The education authority is responsible for making sure that all copies of the Record are also modified.

The education authority may only disclose information in the Record of Needs to certain specified categories of people. On request, they must disclose relevant information to the Scottish Ministers, the named person or the Scottish Children's Reporter Administration where it is needed for the exercise of their functions.

The education authority may also disclose information from the Record (not including the section detailing your views on recording), if it is satisfied that it is for a reasonable purpose to any of the following:

- a teacher concerned with your child's special educational needs;
- the social work department;
- the health board;
- anyone conducting educational, medical or social research (in this case the information will be anonymous); or
- any other person (with your written permission).

Copies of the Record provided by the education authority are returnable on demand. This does not apply to your copy.

After the Record of Needs has been discontinued it is usually kept by the education authority for 5 years. It is then destroyed.

Data Protection

The law gives individuals rights in respect of personal information held on computer or as part of a "relevant filing system" (i.e. including paper records). This includes educational records.

You, as an individual, have a right to access any information about yourself. If your child is too young to make his/her own request, you can make it on their behalf. You must make a request in writing (including e-mail) and pay a fee (which should not exceed £10).

Within 40 days of your request, the "data controller" (in this case the school or education authority) must tell you what information it has about you, why it has it and to whom it is being disclosed. You should also receive a copy of the information and any further information needed to be able to make sense of it. For example, if the school uses abbreviations or codes, a key should be provided. You should also be told where the information came from.

The above rights do not apply to Records of Needs. Nor do they apply where disclosure would allow another individual to be identified, unless they have consented or it would otherwise be reasonable to disclose the information.

If you think that the data controller is not complying with your request properly, you can apply to court for an order to force them to. You can also complain to the Information Commissioner.

If you think that information held about your child is factually inaccurate, you can apply to the court for an order to correct or erase the inaccurate information. You may also be entitled to compensation if the error has caused damage (i.e. financial or educational) to you or your child.

If you have a complaint about the way information is being handled or about a request for access to that information, you may ask the Information Commissioner to investigate. If she finds any wrongdoing, she may serve information notices, requiring the school or education authority to put things right. This may lead to further enforcement action.

See also

Special Educational Needs

Legal references used in this section

The **Data Protection Act 1998**

The **School Pupil Records (Scotland) Regulations 1990**

Reg 4; 6; 7; 8; 9 of the **Education (Record of Needs) (Scotland) Regulations 1982**

Reg 10 of the **Schools General (Scotland) Regulations 1975**

Data Protection (miscellaneous Subject Access Exemptions) Order 2000

SCHOOL RULES

The education authority has a duty to ensure that its schools develop in their pupils:

> reasonable and responsible relationships,
> initiative and self reliance,
> consideration for others,
> good manners and attitude to work, and
> habits of personal hygiene and cleanliness.

These will usually be reflected in the school's rules. Each school has its own set of rules which your child is expected to obey.

What if I don't agree with the school rules?

You are expected to encourage compliance with the school rules. Failing to allow your child to comply with them is one of the grounds for exclusion from school. Your child's failure to follow school rules may lead to further sanctions in accordance with the school rules. If it is felt that the level of non-compliance would be seriously detrimental to order and discipline in the school, then this may lead to your child's exclusion. A statement of the school rules (although not the full rules) must be included in the written information about the school given to parents before their child starts there.

See also

Exclusion from school

Legal references used in this section

Reg. 11 of the **Schools General (Scotland) Regulations 1975**

SCHOOL STARTING AGE (including deferred entry)

Children normally start school when they are aged 4 or 5. The education authority will set a "school commencement date" for each year. This date is important for two reasons. Firstly, it determines when children legally become of "school age" and secondly, it determines which children the education authority is obliged to offer school places to in a particular session.

All children who are aged 5 at the school commencement date are legally of school age and their parents are under an obligation to provide them with an education. This applies whether you intend sending your child to a local authority school or educating him/her in some other way.

The education authority must make a place available at a school for a child who is aged 4 at the school commencement date, but who will have turned 5 by the "appropriate latest date". The appropriate latest date is a date again set by the education authority. There cannot be a gap of more than 6 months and 7 days between the appropriate latest date for one session and the school commencement date for the following session. A parent whose child's 5th birthday falls between the school commencement date and the latest appropriate date has the option to either send the child to school while they are still 4, or to defer entry until the following session when they have turned 5.

If a child turns 5 between the appropriate latest date for one session and the school commencement date for the following session, they must normally wait until the following session to start school, although if your child turns 5 after the appropriate latest date, you can ask the education authority for a place in a primary school. If the education provided at that school is suited to the ability and aptitude of your child, then the education authority must provide him/her with a place.

THE SCOTTISH PARLIAMENT AND SCOTTISH EXECUTIVE

The Scottish Parliament

Following the referendum on devolution in 1997, the Scotland Act 1998 established the Scottish Parliament. The first elections to the Scottish Parliament took place in 1999 and elections must take place every 4 years.

The Scottish Parliament has the power to make new laws for Scotland. However, there are restrictions on its "legislative competence" (i.e. the laws it is allowed to make):

> Firstly, it is not allowed to legislate on "reserved matters", which are reserved to Westminster. These include defence, social security, employment, and consumer protection, among some other things. Education is not a reserved matter and so the Scottish Parliament can make laws relating to Education. In fact one of the first statutes it enacted was the Standards in Scotland's Schools etc (Scotland) Act 2000.

> Secondly, it can only make laws which are compatible with the European Convention on Human Rights.

If the Scottish Parliament made a law that was outwith its legislative competence, it would not be a law at all. If a court is considering a case, and the issue of whether an Act of the Scottish Parliament is within its legislative competence, this is called a "devolution issue." The Advocate General and the Lord Advocate must be told about any devolution issues and be given the opportunity to become involved in the case. Courts can refer devolution issues to the Inner House of the Court of Session or the High Court for a decision.

The Scottish Executive

The Scottish Executive is the equivalent of the Westminster cabinet. Its members include the First Minister and the Ministers appointed by him/her. The Scottish Executive is known collectively as the Scottish Ministers. The Scottish Ministers have administrative back up from civil servants who work in the Scottish Executive. The Scottish Executive is split into departments and the Scottish Executive Education Department (SEED) is responsible for administering government policy in relation to a wide range of areas involving children and young people, including education, social work and youth justice.

To this end, SEED issues guidance and circulars on education matters and funds research into related issues. It funds various non-departmental public bodies, such as the Scottish Children's Reporter Administration. HM Inspectorate of Education is part of the SEED.

SEX EDUCATION

Sex education is seen as an integral part of a child's personal, social and health education. The Scottish Executive must issue guidance to education authorities on the manner in which sex education should be conducted, and education authorities must have regard to this. The guidance which has been issued outlines the purpose of sex education as being "to provide knowledge and understanding of the nature of sexuality and the processes of human reproduction within the context of relationships based on love and respect." There is to be an emphasis on the importance of commitment, and respect in relationships, and on the responsibilities of both partners in a sexual relationship. It is also important to bear in mind in this context the general duty of a local authority in the performance of its functions which relate principally to children, to have regard to

> the value of stable family life in a child's development; and

> the need to ensure that the content of instruction provided in the performance of those functions is appropriate, having regard to each child's age, understanding and stage of development

Government guidance states that schools should consult parents and carers when developing their sex education programmes, and parents and carers should have the opportunity to examine the materials which will be used, in advance.

If you have concerns about what your child will be taught, you should make an appointment with the head teacher, who will explain the purpose of sex education, and will go over what your child will be taught. If you are still not happy with your child attending these classes, you can withdraw your child from them. If you decide to do this, your child should be given an alternative class to attend while his/her classmates are receiving sex education. Matters relating to sex, sexuality and morality may come up in other classes within the curriculum. However it is not possible to have your child withdrawn from classes where these matters *may* arise.

If you have concerns about the information or materials your child has been given, you should take this up with the head teacher in the first instance. If you are not satisfied with the response, you are also able to take the matter up with the education authority.

See also

Curriculum (what is taught)

Where to find out more

"*Sex Education in Scottish Schools: a guide for parents and carers*" by Learning and Teaching Scotland. Also available on the Parent Zone web site.

Legal references used in this section

Section 56 of the **Standards in Scotland's Schools etc. (Scotland) Act 2000**

Section 35 of the **Ethical Standards in Public Life etc. (Scotland) Act 2000**

Scottish Executive Circular 2/2001

SPECIAL ABILITIES AND APTITUDES

Your child may have special talents or aptitudes in specific subjects which may require additional attention to fully develop.

The education authority must provide you with information about its policies and practices for educating children with special talents. The Scottish Executive, through the Excellence Fund has made available funds to set up and support schools which cater for children with special talents in particular subjects, such as sport, music, traditional music, dance and international languages. Study may be available by way of distance learning, or in the evening and at weekends. Intake to such schools is limited and is based on merit.

The education authority has a general duty to provide an adequate and efficient education and must have regard to your child's aptitudes and abilities. That education must also be directed to developing your child's personality, talents and mental and physical abilities to their fullest potential. The education authority has powers to make available special educational provision in exceptional circumstances, which might be used if required to provide appropriate provision for a child with special abilities or aptitude.

There will be opportunities for your child to take additional tuition in courses, lessons and other activities outside the regular school curriculum. Whether you have to pay for these is at the discretion of the education authority. Where you are in dispute with the education authority on this matter, you may consider complaining to the Scottish Ministers or even court action.

See also

Complaints
Legal action

Where to find out more

"A Bright Start" by Edward Chitham. National Association for Gifted Children (1999).

National Association for Gifted Children in Scotland

Legal references used in this section

Section 2(1) of the **Standards in Scotland's Schools etc. (Scotland) Act 2000**

Section 1; 50(1)(b) and 70 of the **Education (Scotland) Act 1980**

Schedule I, Part III (o) of the **Education (Schools and Placing Information) (Scotland) Regulations 1982**

SPECIAL EDUCATIONAL NEEDS

The law about children with special educational needs is part of Education Law as a whole. All the rights and duties that you, your child and the education authority have apply just as much to children with special educational needs. The law does, however, provide for children's special educational needs to be met by the education authority.

Basic Duties of the education authority

The education authority has a duty to ensure that, within its area, "adequate and efficient" provision is made for school education. School education has to be suitable to your child's needs, taking into account their age, aptitude and ability, including any special educational needs.

The education authority must publicise the importance of identifying special educational needs at an early stage. It must also let you know that assessment is available for that purpose.

The education authority must provide written information on its general policy and practice with regard to provision in schools for pupils with special educational needs. Each special school must also provide information about the types of need catered for and specialist services provided.

For all children of school age and any children over the age of 2 who have apparent special educational needs, the education authority must identify which children have "pronounced, specific or complex" special educational needs which require continuing review. It must open a Record of Needs for each child who does. It *may* also do so for any pre-school child or young person (with their permission).

Special Educational Needs

About 20% of all school children have some form of special educational needs and about 2% have a Record of Needs.

Your child has special educational needs if he/she has a learning difficulty which means he/she needs special educational provision. It need not be caused by a disability.

Your child has a learning difficulty if he/she:

(a) finds learning significantly more difficult than most other children of the same age; or

(b) has a disability which prevents or hinders him/her from making use of educational facilities provided at the schools in the area for children of that age; or

(c) is under 5 but is likely to come under (a) or (b) once they reach 5, or would if no action is taken now.

For example, pupils with dyslexia are likely to have special educational needs. Pupils who require speech therapy also have special educational needs. It is an educational need, as well as a medical one. Your child may have special educational needs due to a prolonged absence from school. However, your child will not have special educational needs simply because he/she does not speak or understand English, because this is not caused by a disability.

Observation and Assessment

Once identified, your child must be assessed in accordance with the very detailed procedures laid down by law. These include an obligation to take into account your views as a parent.

Initiated by the education authority

The observation and assessment process leading to possible recording will often begin with a request made by the education authority to you to allow your child to be assessed. This is done by way of written notice.

The purpose of the assessment is to provide the education authority with information and recommendations about your child's special educational needs and whether or not he/she should be recorded. You have a statutory right to be present at any <u>medical</u> examination required for the assessment. You may have a common law right to be present during the rest of the assessment process too.

You must be invited to give your views on your child's special educational needs and any measures required to meet those needs. You must give your views in writing within 21 days of the date of the written notice (some education authorities allow longer).

If your child does not attend the assessment (without a reasonable excuse) and he/she is at least two years old, then another notice will be served on you, compelling you to send your child for assessment. If you do not, you are committing an offence, and the education authority is released from its duty of observation and assessment for your child.

Initiated by the parent

If you request an assessment for your child (who is at least two years old), the education authority must comply (unless your request is unreasonable). The education authority must assess the child unless there are very good reasons for refusing.

A young person must be invited to express his/her views on their special educational needs and measures required to meet those needs. Their parent must be invited to do so where the young person is incapable of expressing their own views for these purposes.

The assessment will usually be co-ordinated by the education authority's educational psychologist. However, it will also include reports from others who contribute to the assessment, looking at different aspects of your child's needs. The assessment must consider medical, educational and psychological reports. It must also include your views. A young person's own views must be included (or yours as the case may be). If other relevant reports are available (e.g. from a speech therapist) then they too must be considered.

The right to give your views can include the submission of independent reports, and the views of others e.g. siblings and other relatives, or carers. On the basis of the assessment, the education authority makes a decision about whether or not to open a Record of Needs.

The decision to record

Before making a decision to record (or not), the education authority must take into account:

- the advice given following observation & assessment;
- any views expressed by you, or your child (if old enough);
- any reports or other information available from the managers or teachers at schools he/she has attended; and
- any other reports or information it is able to obtain.

You will receive written notice of the education authority's decision about recording, together with the reasons for the decision and a draft record (if your child is to be recorded). You then have 14 days to give your views on the draft.

The education authority must take account of your views. It must then notify you of the final decision and of your rights of appeal.

An education authority may be liable if there is a failure to diagnose correctly, or provide for your child's special educational needs. Where such failure affects your child's educational attainment and/or employability, the education authority may have to compensate him/her.

The Record of Needs

A Record of Needs consists of:

Part I   name, address and personal details of your child;
Part II   your name and address and those of the Named Person;

Part IIIa the assessment profile – a brief description of your child;

Part IIIb a summary of his/her impairments;

Part IV a statement of the special educational needs arising from your child's impairments;

Part V a statement of what the education authority will do to meet these needs;

Part VI the school to be attended;

Part VII your views or those of your child (if old enough);

Part VIII a summary of any reviews of the Record;

Part IX information listing people who have access to the Record.

The Record should follow in a logical sequence. Parts I to III should be drawn from the assessment which has been carried out. Part III should form the basis of Parts IV and V. This will help decide which school should be in Part VI.

A Record of Needs must detail and make provision for each and every difficulty identified.

Part V of the Record should state what resources and support the education authority will provide, and detail any arrangements to obtain services from other organisations (such as the health board). The legal obligation for providing the services in Part V lies with the education authority, regardless of who actually delivers it. This obligation can be enforced through the courts, if necessary.

Part V should be specific enough for the school to be able to draw up an individualised educational programme (IEP) for your child. An IEP gives specific guidance on:

curricular activities;
teaching and learning resources;
teaching and learning strategies for your child.

However, the IEP has no legal status, is not binding on the education authority and is **not** a substitute for a Record of Needs. If your child has "pronounced, specific or complex" special educational needs which require continuing review, then he/she is entitled to a Record of Needs, and the education authority <u>must</u> record.

Rights of appeal

For more detailed information about making an appeal, see also **Appeals**.

Certain decisions made by the education authority about Records of Need may be referred to an education appeal committee, composed of 3, 5 or 7 members, being a mix of councillors and parents.

You may appeal against any of the following decisions:

- to record your child or to continue their Record on review;
- not to record your child or to discontinue their Record on review;
- the summary of your child's impairments (part IIIb);
- the special educational needs arising from those impairments (part IV);
- the nomination of school to be attended (part VI); and
- the refusal of a placing request.

A young person (or as the case may be, you as their parent) may appeal against the following decisions:

- not to record them or to discontinue their Record on review;
- the summary of their impairments;
- the special educational needs arising from those impairments;
- the nomination of school to be attended; and
- the refusal of a placing request.

An appeal against a nominated school can only be made if you or your child (if old enough) have made a placing request also. Once an appeal against a nominated school or against a refusal of a placing request is made, you cannot make another appeal for 12 months.

If you want to make an appeal, you have 28 days from receiving the decision you disagree with to refer it to the education appeal committee. The committee can hear late appeals if there is a good reason. The education appeal committee refers all appeals (other than those relating to choice of school) to the Scottish Ministers for a decision. The Scottish Ministers will make a decision, having obtained and taken into account your views. There is then no further right of appeal.

The appeal committee deals with appeals relating to choice of school itself. A decision of the appeal committee is subject to further appeal to the Sheriff Court, by way of "summary application". The decision of the court is final. An appeal to the court, while kept as informal as possible, is a complex legal procedure, and you should seek legal advice and/or representation from a solicitor familiar with education law. You may be entitled to Legal Aid, and your child almost certainly will be.

The appeal at the Sheriff Court is heard as a rehearing of the whole case, and the court can reverse the decision of the appeal committee if it is "appropriate" to do so.

Placing requests and choice of school

If your child has "pronounced, specific or complex" special educational needs, the education authority can (but does not have to) enable him/her to attend an educational establishment which caters for his/her needs outwith the United Kingdom. Payment may be made for fees and other expenses, for your child and also for you, if you need to be with him/her.

If your child is a recorded pupil and you make a written request to the education authority to place your child in a specified school, the education authority must comply with your request unless one of the normal exceptions for placing requests applies, or:

• where the specified school is an independent school in the United Kingdom and your child does not have special educational needs requiring the education or special facilities normally provided for at that school; or

- the education authority is able to make provision for the special educational needs of the child in a school under its management; and

- it is not reasonable, considering the suitability and cost of provision for the special educational needs of your child, to place him/her in the specified school; and

- the education authority has offered to place your child in the school under its management.

Where the specified school is an independent special school which is prepared to admit your child, or it is a school in England & Wales or Northern Ireland which is prepared to admit your child, and it makes provision wholly or mainly for children or young people with pronounced, specific or complex special educational needs, then the education authority must meet all fees and other necessary costs of attendance at that school (e.g. uniforms, travel, materials etc.). If you can show that an independent school would best meet your child's needs, the education authority must comply, subject to the above rules.

A change in the law is shortly to be introduced, giving a statutory presumption that children with special educational needs will be educated within mainstream schools, except in exceptional circumstances. It is further stated that such exceptional circumstances will occur only exceptionally! This will have major implications for mainstream and special needs education alike, but at the time of going to press it was unclear how this would be implemented.

Transport

The education authority must meet the costs of transport to the school recommended in the Record of Needs. Where a successful placing request has been made, but the nominated school is unchanged, the education authority need not meet the travel costs unless the school in question is an independent special school in Scotland; or a special school outwith Scotland.

Review of the Record of Needs

A Record of Needs is not a static document. It must be kept under consideration and review. The education authority must review its decision to record and the information entered in the Record if it thinks it should, or if it is asked to do so in writing by you (or by a young person). Such a request can only be made once every twelve months. A review should be handled as if it were an original assessment. You have the same rights of appeal to the education appeal committee again.

Transition to adulthood (the Future Needs Assessment)

Statutory provisions exist which try to make sure there is a smooth hand-over of responsibility from the education department (responsible for special educational provision) to the social work department (responsible for the continuing community care needs) of the disabled child (where this is applicable).

The education authority must consider what provision would benefit each recorded child when he/she reaches school leaving age. This must be done no more than 2 years and no less than 9 months before then. The process can be carried out in conjunction with a review, generally known as a Future Needs Assessment, and is similar to an original assessment.

The resulting report must be sent to you. It should include a recommendation about whether your child would benefit from remaining in school after school leaving age and, if so, whether the Record should be discontinued at that age. It must also tell you about your right to have the Record discontinued. If appropriate, the local health board will be sent a copy as will, with your consent, any other body making provision from which your child might benefit (which can include further education establishments). The social work department will also receive a copy. This procedure is essentially aimed at allowing smooth transition for your child into adult life.

The education authority must continue the Record once your child reaches school leaving age for as long as he/she remains in school, unless your child (or you) asks for it to be discontinued.

See also

Placing requests

Where to find out more

Enquire

Independent Special Education Advice Scotland

"The Parents' Guide to Special Educational Needs" by Children in Scotland and the Scottish Executive Education Department (2000).

"Special Educational Needs" Subject Map by the Scottish Parliament (April 2000).

"Your future needs assessment" by Children in Scotland.

Legal references used in this section

Section 15 of the **Standards in Scotland's Schools etc. (Scotland) Act 2000**

Section 1; 28F; 60; 61; 62; 63; 65 A, B, C & G; Schedule A2 of the **Education (Scotland) Act 1980**

Education (Record of Needs) (Scotland) Regulations 1982

Schedule I, Part II(f) and III(p) of the **Education (Schools and Placing Information) (Scotland) Regulations 1982**

E. (A Minor) v. Dorset County Council [1994] ELR 416

R v. Secretary of State for Education and Science, ex parte E. [1992] 1 FLR 316

See R v. Lancashire County Council, ex parte C.M. (A Minor) (1989) Fam. Law 395

R v. Hampshire County Council, ex parte J. The Times December 5, 1985

See R v. Hampshire Education Authority, ex parte J. (1985) 84 LGR 547

STANDARDS IN SCHOOL EDUCATION

At a national level

There is now an obligation on the Scottish Ministers to try to improve the quality of education in Scotland. When making decisions about educational provision, they must have this in mind. They must also set national priorities for educational objectives in school education. (They will consult education authorities and other bodies in setting these priorities). The first national priorities have now been set and include raising literacy and numeracy levels, enhancing school environments, and developing self respect and respect for others in school pupils.

At education authority level

Education authorities, too, have a duty to try to improve the quality of school education in their area, and must make an "annual statement of education improvement objectives". This must include a description of:

• How the authority will involve parents in promoting the education of their children;

• How it encourages equal opportunities;

• The circumstances in which it will provide Gaelic medium education

and will set objectives relating to the national priorities in education (and other matters as the education authority sees fit).

Each education authority must then publish an annual report on how well it has achieved the objectives it has set itself. The date for the first report has yet to be set but is expected to be sometime in 2002-3.

Schools too have responsibilities in improving the standards in education, and head teachers, on behalf of the education authority must prepare a "school development plan" for their school, setting out the objectives for that school in meeting the education authority's own annual statement of education improvement objectives. Teachers and parents are consulted about what should be in the school development plan. Then an annual report is published on what was done to implement the plan. Copies of the development plan and the annual report should be made available free of charge to parents.

Where to find out more

"Attendance and Absence in Scottish Schools" by the Scottish Executive (current edition).

"Examination Results in Scottish Schools" by the Scottish Executive (current edition).

"Destinations of Leavers from Scottish Secondary Schools" by the Scottish Executive (current edition).

"Scottish Schools: costs" by the Scottish Executive (current edition).

"Raising Standards: Setting Targets - setting targets in Scottish schools. National and Education Authority Information" by the Scottish Executive (1999).

Legal references used in this section

Sections 3-8 of the **Standards in Scotland's Schools etc (Scotland) Act 2000**

TEACHERS' CONDITIONS OF SERVICE

Teachers' terms of employment

The conditions under which teachers are employed are mainly governed by national-level negotiation between the teaching profession and local authorities. The Scottish Negotiating Committee for Teachers is made up of representatives of the teaching unions, local authorities and the Scottish Executive. They cover matters like teachers' working hours; how much class teaching is done; grievance and discipline procedures; absences and other matters. Some other matters will be decided locally.

These arrangements do not apply to teachers in independent schools.

Teachers are also bound by the terms of the contract of employment with their employers. This includes the express written terms and certain other duties implied at common law into contracts of employment. For example there is a general duty on teachers to obey all reasonable instructions given by their employers.

Teachers' qualifications

These are the qualifications which teachers must normally have if trained in Scotland:

- Primary teachers must hold either a degree in primary education or a Post Graduate Certificate in Education;

- Secondary teachers must hold a university degree in a relevant subject and a Post Graduate Certificate in Education, or a degree in their chosen subject which includes a teaching qualification.

Under European Law, teachers with equivalent teaching qualifications from other EU countries must be allowed to teach in UK schools.

Once qualified, in order to teach in a local authority school, all teachers must register with the General Teaching Council for Scotland. Registration is not legally *required* for teaching in independent schools, although in practice, most independent schools do insist on registration. Teachers are registered provisionally at first, until they complete a probationary period satisfactorily. At present the probationary period is two years, but it is proposed that this be reduced to one year. At any stage in a teacher's career, registration can be withdrawn as a result of criminal conviction or professional misconduct.

Working hours

Under a new agreement, teachers' working week will be 35 hours, excluding lunch and breaks. Class contact time is to be reduced to 22½ hours per week by August 2006. In the meantime, teachers are entitled to a weekly allowance of time not less than one-third of class contact time, for preparation and marking. Any tasks which do not require a teacher's physical presence at the school can be carried out at the time and place of his/her choosing.

Teachers do not have to take part in activities outside of school time, such as school clubs or sports fixtures.

Industrial action

Teachers have the same rights as other employees in an industrial dispute, and are very unlikely to be dismissed for participating in an official strike. During industrial action, the education authority has a legal obligation to take whatever reasonable steps are necessary to ensure that services are kept running where possible. Where an education authority is not taking adequate steps to ensure your child's access to education during an industrial dispute, you could complain to the Scottish Ministers or take legal action. The Scottish Ministers or the court would then have to decide whether, in view of the industrial action, the education authority had nonetheless acted reasonably in fulfilling or attempting to fulfil its duties to provide your child with school education.

Where possible, the school must inform you of industrial action before it takes place so that you can make alternative arrangements for your child if he/she is not to attend school.

See also

Complaints
Legal action

Legal references used in this section

Section 70 of the **Education (Scotland) Act 1980**

The European Communities (Recognition of Professional Qualifications) Regulations 1991, provides for the recognition of the qualifications of teachers from other EU countries.

TRANSPORT

The education authority must, when necessary, arrange transport for pupils to get to school and back. Transport may be provided by the education authority's own buses or contracted transport. Taxis and private cars are often used. In more remote areas, ferries and even aircraft are sometimes used. The law specifically mentions providing bicycles for pupils to use, but there are not thought to be any examples of this in practice.

Written information about transport arrangements must be provided to parents, including entitlement to free school transport where available.

Free school transport

Free school transport must be provided for children who live further than the "statutory walking distance" away from the school. This is:

> For pupils under 8 years old, two miles;
> For pupils aged 8 or more, three miles.

This does not apply if your child attends a school other than the local school (or other school nominated by the education authority) because you made a placing request. Then you will have to make your own arrangements for travel.

Neither does it apply to nursery or pre-school education, although the education authority may provide assistance or transport if it wants.

Free school transport does not have to be provided for the whole distance, so long as the distance your child needs to walk is less than the statutory walking distance. So, for example, there may be a walk from the house to the bus stop and a walk from the bus stop to the school, which can be anything up to 2 or 3 miles.

In remote areas, the education authority may offer boarding accommodation in hostels provided and maintained for pupils rather than transport.

Lack of suitable transport is listed as a potential reasonable excuse for non-attendance at school. This may apply where the route, though shorter than the statutory walking distance, is hazardous or otherwise unsuitable for children. In these circumstances, the education authority still has an obligation to provide education for your child. The simplest way of meeting this obligation is by providing free transport.

The education authority has discretion to offer free transport to any pupil. It must offer spare places on a school bus to pupils who would otherwise not be entitled to the free school transport. These "courtesy places" may have to be given up if the number of pupils entitled to free transport increases. The education authority should give adequate notice to allow alternative arrangements to be made if this affects your child. It may also have to allow a period of consultation.

There are special rules for children with special educational needs.

Safety on school transport

The education authority is responsible for the safety and (where appropriate) supervision of pupils on transport it provides as above. This is the case even where the vehicle itself is provided by a private company, although they may share some of the responsibility.

See also

Consulting parents
Special educational needs

Where to find out more

"Safe School Travel" by the Scottish School Board Association (1998).

Legal references used in this section

Section 37 of the **Standards in Scotland's Schools etc. (Scotland) Act 2000**

Section 13; 42(1)&(4); 50(1)&(2); 51(4); of the **Education (Scotland) Act 1980**

Schools (Safety and Supervision of Pupils) (Scotland) Regulations 1990

Schedule I Part II(l) of the **Education (Schools and Placing Information) (Scotland) Regulations 1982**

USEFUL ADDRESSES

Childline Scotland
18 Albion Street
Glasgow G1 14H
0141 552 1123
www.childlinescotland.org.uk

Children in Scotland
Princes House
5 Shandwick Place
Edinburgh EH2 4RG
0131 228 8484
www.childreninscotland.org.uk

Citizens Advice Scotland
26 George Square
Edinburgh
0131 667 0156
www.cas.org.uk

Commission for Racial Equality
Elliot House
10-12 Allington Street
London SW1E 5EH
0207 828 7022
www.cre.gov.uk

Consumers Association
2 Marylebone Road
London NW1 4DX
0207 830 6000
www.which.net

CoSLA (Convention of Scottish Local Authorities)
Rosebery House
9 Haymarket Terrace
Edinburgh EH12 5XZ
0131 474 9200
www.cosla.gov.uk

Disability Rights Commission
Freepost MID 02164
Stratford-upon-Avon CV37 9BR
08457 622633
www.drc-gb.org/drc/default.asp

Enable
7 Buchanan Street
Glasgow G1 3HL
0141 226 4541

Enquire Helpline
0131 2222 400

Equal Opportunities Commission
St Stevens House
279 Bath Street
Glasgow G2 4JL
0141 248 5833

European Court of Human Rights
www.echr.coe.int

General Teaching Council for Scotland
Clerwood House
96 Clermiston Road
Edinburgh EH12 6UT
0131 314 6000
www.gtcs.org.uk

HM Inspectorate of Education (HMIE)
Saughton House
Broomhouse Drive
Edinburgh EH11 3XD
0131 244 0650/8293
www.scotland.gov.uk/hmie

HMSO
St Clements House
2-16 Colegate
Norwich NR3 1BQ
01603 621000
www.hmso.gov.uk

Independent Schools Information Service
21 Melville Street
Edinburgh EH3 7PG
0131 220 2706
www.isis.org.uk

Independent Special Education Advice (ISEA)
164 High Street
Dalkeith
Midlothian EH22 1AY
0131 454 0082

Information Commissioner
Wycliffe House
Water Lane
Wilmslow
Cheshire SK9 5AF
01625 545 700
www.dataprotection.gov.uk

Law Society of Scotland
26 Drumsheugh Gardens
Edinburgh EH3 7YR
0131 476 8137
www.lawscot.org.uk

Learning and Teaching Scotland
74 Victoria Crescent Road
Glasgow G12 9JN
0141 337 5000
www.ltscotland.com

Local Government Ombudsman
23 Walker Street
Edinburgh EH3 7HX
0131 225 5300
http://www.ombudslgscot.org.uk/

National Association for Gifted Children
01908 673 677
www.nagcbritain.org.uk

National Association for Gifted Children in Scotland
www.school-resources.co.uk/national_association_for_gifted_.htm

National Children's Bureau
8 Wakely Street
London EC1V 7QE
0207 843 6000
www.ncb.org.uk

Parentline Scotland
41 Polwarth Terrace
Edinburgh
EH11 1NU
0808 800 222

Parent Zone
www.ngflscotland.gov.uk/parentzone

Save the Children
17 Grove Lane
London SE5 8RD
0207 703 5400
www.savethechildren.org.uk

Schoolhouse Home Education Association
311 Perth Road
Dundee DD2 12G
0870 745 0968
www.schoolhouse.org.uk

Scottish Anti-Bullying Network
Moray House Institute of Education
University of Edinburgh
Holyrood Road
Edinburgh EH8 8AQ
0131 651 6100
www.antibullying.net

Scottish Association of Law Centres
Dalsetter Avenue
Glasgow G15
0141 445 6451

Scottish Child Law Centre
23 Buccleugh Place
Edinburgh EH8 9LN
0131 667 6333

Scottish Committee of the council of Tribunals
44 Palmerston Place
Edinburgh EH12 5BJ
0131 220 1236
www.council-on-tribunals.gov.uk/scottish.htm

Scottish Council of Independent Schools
21 Melville Street
Edinburgh EH3 7PE
0131 225 8594
www.scis.org.uk

Scottish Council for Research in Education
15 St John Street
Edinburgh EH8 8JR
0131 557 2944
www.scre.ac.uk

Scottish Executive Education Department
Victoria Quay
Edinburgh EH6 6QQ
0131 556 8400
www.scotland.gov.uk/who/dept_education.asp

Scottish Human Rights Centre
146 Holland Street
Glasgow G2 4NG
0141 332 5960
www.shrc.dial.pipex.com

Scottish Parent Teacher Council
63/65 Shandwick Place
Edinburgh
EH2 4SD
0131 228 5320
http://www.sol.co.uk/s/sptc

Scottish Parliament
Edinburgh EH99 1SP
0131 348 5000
www.scottish.parliament.uk

Scottish Qualifications Authority
Hanover House
24 Douglas Street
Glasgow G2 7NQ
0845 279 1000
www.sqa.org.uk

Scottish Refugee Council
98 West George Street
Glasgow G2 1PJ
0141 333 1850
www.scottishrefugeecouncil.org.uk

Scottish School Board Association
Newall Terrace
Dumfries DG1 1LW
01387 260428
www.schoolboard-scotland.com

Skill: National Bureau for Students with Disabilities
Norton Park
57 Albion Road
Edinburgh EH7 5QY
0131 475 2348
www.skill.org.uk

The Stationery Office
73 Lothian Road
Edinburgh
EH3 9AW
www.thestationeryoffice.com
www.clicktso.com

The Stationery Office
51 Nine Elms Lane
London SW8 5DR
www.thestationeryoffice.com
www.clicktso.com

Student Awards Agency for Scotland
Gyleview House
3 Redheughs Rigg
Edinburgh EH12 9HH
0131 476 8212
www.saas.org.uk

Student Loans Company
100 Bothwell Street
Glasgow G2 7JD
www.slc.co.uk

Universities and Colleges Admission Services (UCAS)
Rosehill
New Barn Lane
Cheltenham
Gloucestershire GL52 3LZ
01242 222444
www.ucas.ac.uk